For Isobel and Lily
And for DH

Also by Lucy Rocca

How To Lead a Happier, Healthier and Alcohol-Free Life

Glass Half Full

The Sober Revolution – Calling Time on Wine O'Clock

Your Six-Week Plan – Join the Sober Revolution and Call Time on Wine O'Clock

Introduction

Who knows what led you to picking up this book? You might consider yourself to be a binge-drinker, a frequent drinker, an out-of-control drinker, an alcoholic, a boozer, someone who likes a drink ... perhaps you had a major blowout last night and you know that you have to end this merry-go-round, or maybe the drunken arguments are becoming too frequent and too awful to endure any longer. Whatever the reason, and whatever the definition you ascribe to your tendency to consume alcohol in excess, you need to know right now that it's not your fault. It is not your fault. It. Is. Not. Your. Fault.

The western world is really a terribly boozy place. Everyone loves to drink, don't they? Drinking is not just acceptable but encouraged, expected, revered. But there are hundreds of thousands of people in the UK alone who are off the scale in terms of how hazardous their drinking has become; who binge-drink as a means of feeling sociable, less stressed, or to tune out their surroundings momentarily. And a large proportion of these people will blame themselves and continue to booze away their concerns in private, struggling to cope with the regular mornings of self-hatred and ruinous hangovers, too scared and ashamed to ask for help.

I was one of those people until a few years ago.

It's now been more than five years since I had my last alcoholic drink, and I love *not drinking* far more than I ever loved drinking. Which is saying something, and a statement you'd be rather stunned by if you had known me as a booze hound.

In the last few years of my alcohol-fuelled life, getting pissed had wormed its way into every crevice, nook and cranny of my existence. All my spare time was geared towards, or had at its heart, booze – especially wine. If I wasn't drinking then I was looking forward to drinking, or recovering from it, or planning an event that allowed for it in large quantities. And it struck me, aged as I was then in my mid-thirties, that this was a tragically sad way to spend my life: being a slave to an addictive substance, enabling it to colour the person I was inside and alter (for the worse) my expectations of the future and the opinion I had of myself.

But, despite this growing sense that alcohol was no longer working for me, I was hampered by the belief that in some way this was all my fault – that I was to blame for my obvious inability to control this stuff that most of the population was pouring down its neck every night without, apparently, a care in the world. I had turned into a dreaded 'problem drinker', complete with the reputation of being a liability – one to watch on a night out due to my routine acts of passing out, flirting outrageously with all and sundry and throwing up all over the pub toilets.

But let's get one thing straight – the blame I allotted to myself for the unhealthy development of my relationship with alcohol did nothing whatsoever to help me get things sorted. I soon realised, once I'd made the brilliant decision to quit drinking altogether, that the wellness process would be sped up nicely if only I could simultaneously learn to be kind to myself and come to appreciate the good to be found in being sober – all of the time.

So I set to work restructuring myself from the inside out – how I perceived life; how I perceived alcohol; my choice of friends and partner; how I spent my spare time; how I treated myself; the messages I told myself about who I was and what I deserved out of life. I brainwashed myself a fair bit with self-help books, and I got off my backside and threw myself into exercising and learning how to meditate. I sought comfort in simplicity and wondered at all the incredible things I'd been missing out on for the twenty-two years I had spent getting drunk.

Over the course of the last five years, I have transformed myself from a drunken bum to a happy, healthy and self-respecting individual with no desire whatsoever to drink. I don't blame myself any more for the fact that I found myself unable to control the amount of alcohol I drank. I don't label myself, and I love my life.

I wrote this book, noting all the things I did which got me to this place, as a way to help *you* navigate your own route out of the booze trap, and to remind you that the journey to true happiness begins with learning to love yourself.

That journey starts here – it's time to get well again.

A
Awareness of the Problem

You cannot begin to address any problem unless you first acknowledge that it exists. Personally, I think that admitting you've stepped over the invisible line and become (sshhh!) one of 'them' is right up there among the hardest things to do in the world. Why? Because we live in the Land of the Boozers. Everyone and their grandma likes to drink in the West. Booze is an icebreaker, a leveller; it soothes away social discomfort with the ease of a gentle breeze. With an alcoholic beverage close to hand, people find themselves able to enter into conversation with those they would struggle to utter a single word to when sober.

And yet, if you slide uncontrollably (and probably unknowingly as the transition is occurring) into the realm of alcohol dependency then you are deemed to have parted company from 'us' and entered into the territory of 'them'. And this demarcation of the habits of drinkers, from responsible on the one side to alcoholics on the other, is the biggest hurdle we face when it comes to the title of this chapter – awareness of the problem.

When I was a teenager, I lived close to a mini-market. In the evenings, my friends and I would meet up there and smoke our cigarettes; occasionally swigging from a bottle or two of cheap booze, should we have been able to convince an older friend or sibling to purchase some on our behalf. Just around the corner lived a boy who we went to school with, and every night at about 7 p.m. his mother would stumble down the road and visit the mini-market to buy alcohol. She was what I recognised as an alcoholic – her cheeks were ruddy and she couldn't walk in a straight line. She never smiled, her clothes looked dirty and her face revealed the thinly veiled shame of people who can't control their alcohol consumption. She would totter with an uncertain gait into the shop before re-emerging minutes later, clutching a carrier bag filled with clanking bottles.

We labelled her an 'alkie' and believed her to be different from us – the ones who were downing cheap cider and fortified wines on a street corner. And, as the years passed by, that woman settled into my world view and became the gold standard of what an alcoholic looked like.

Years later, I said to my sister, in all seriousness, 'I'd hate to become an alcoholic because then I'd have to stop drinking.' I failed to detect any irony in this statement at the time, but I often think back to it and almost laugh (not quite) at my complete lack of awareness regarding just how dependent upon alcohol I already was at that stage. I was in my mid-twenties and booze was still a social lubricant to me; a prop that enabled me to switch personalities and live up to my reputation as something of a rebel and a party girl. But I consumed a lot of it, as much as my male friends (if not more), and I would drink only to get drunk. I couldn't see the point otherwise.

I was surrounded by a circle of friends who all drank to excess, and together we socialised in pubs that were occupied exclusively by heavy drinkers. And beyond my immediate social group, I witnessed the majority of the population consuming alcohol regularly too – in real life, on the TV and in films. Drinking was sung about in songs and detailed in books. It was an activity so engrained into popular culture that I never, for one moment, considered not taking part. How could I? I lived in the Land of the Boozers.

In my mid-twenties, I occasionally voiced concerns to my then-husband that I might be an alcoholic, a fear that he wasn't fully able to allay for me. My concerns largely stemmed from the frequently debauched social occasions I enjoyed alongside my girlfriends, when we would down vast quantities of wine on nights out away from our husbands and children. Many a time I would wake up the following morning with a throbbing head and sketchy memories of the previous evening's events, together with the knowledge that I seemingly didn't know when I was drunk and should therefore be calling it a night.

After one such evening, I sat and cried on my husband's knee, sobbing my heart out because I was convinced that I had crossed the line and turned into one of them. He reassured me a little and advised me to cut down, perhaps lay off the booze for a while until I felt better able to control my intake – nonsense advice, of course, for the person with no off-switch. I briefly abstained, in the manner of a pissed off teenager who has been instructed to tidy her bedroom, before persuading myself that I was, in fact, a party animal as opposed to an alcoholic and I had no business adopting the lifestyle of a nun.

It was my interpretation of the word 'alcoholic' that prevented me from truly coming to terms with my drink problem during the twenty-two years I spent binge-drinking on a regular basis. I perceived alcoholism to be an issue troubling them and not us, the latter being the camp to which I felt I firmly belonged. It was, in addition, the general acceptance of what drinking too much, or alcoholism, meant in our society that kept me safe from these dreaded labels. In my mind, drinking was connected to fun times, happy social events and easy flirtation with the opposite sex. It was not, yet, sinister in any way.

Of course, there was a further reason regarding my inability to acknowledge that I was alcohol dependent: in and among the terrible booze-related disasters that repeatedly knocked me sideways, damaging my confidence and self-worth, there were times when drinking was still fun. It made me feel young and sexy and enabled me to socialise, free from any of the awkwardness and shyness that I felt when sober. I cherry-picked the memories. For every terrible night which had soured after too much to drink, there was the counter argument – the evenings filled with laughter and good times and silliness; the nights on which all my responsibilities had drifted off and I'd felt blissfully unanchored once more.

And so the awareness, that fundamental – crucial – acceptance that things had gone too far and my relationship with alcohol had been lost to a place of no return, for me arose primarily out of two issues. It was the balance of alcohol-related good times versus bad times and the latter finally outweighing the former. And it was my understanding that having a problem with alcohol does not necessarily happen only when *all* the wheels of your life fall off. You don't need to be reaching for the spirits at 7 a.m. or losing your job, facing a drink-driving charge or having the Social Services contact you over fears for the welfare of your family. It's not a prerequisite to suffer from withdrawal symptoms because your body is crying out for alcohol. And you don't need to be a sad, lonely person *all* of the time.

In fact, as was the case with me, you may find that nobody around you is fully aware of how much importance you attach to alcohol. You probably won't resemble the woman whom my friends and I used to watch as she stumbled down to the shop every night for her fix of booze, and you more than likely will have at least *some* good times when drinking. Right up until I ditched the bottle permanently, I was still putting on a pretty decent act of a person who 'just liked a drink'. But beneath the veneer, I had my doubts.

I'd frequently begun to experience hangover-induced panic attacks during the days after heavy drinking sessions. I would suffer extreme heart palpitations and breathlessness, once so bad that I was convinced I was having a heart attack. I felt as though my nerves were shot to pieces and I was paranoid about developing cancer or cirrhosis of the liver as a result of my alcohol consumption. Plus, I had made a complete arse out of myself on numerous occasions when drunk – snogging people I didn't actually like all that much, falling over, being sick and initiating pointless arguments with those I really cared for.

These factors were gradually accumulating and tipping the balance away from drinking and towards me becoming teetotal. But I still doubted whether or not I really had a booze problem; whether things were so bad that I needed to stop for good. All around me I could see people drinking to excess, way more than was recommended in the government guidelines. And none of them seemed to care. They generally laughed off any drunken misdemeanours and just put them down to having 'one too many'.

But I couldn't shake the feeling of being deeply ashamed of myself as a result of the effects alcohol had upon me. Drinking turned me into a monster. It made me throw up in my sleep. Snap at my daughter. Almost lose my dog. Argue with people. Fall into the bath and bang my head. Collapse on the pavement. Slip down a steep, muddy bank in the dark. Smoke way too many fags. Eat crap. Throw myself out of a moving car. Jeopardise my studies, and later my job. Sleep with people I wasn't all that bothered about. Chuck a pint of beer over someone. Flirt with other men blatantly in front of boyfriends. Shout. Cry. Be depressed. Have panic attacks. Hide in the house, fearful of innocent interactions with people.

None of these alone was sufficient to turn me against alcohol permanently, but many of them resulted in me going on the wagon for a period of a few weeks at a time. Each one contributed to the bank of shame that continued to fester inside, and every morning, when I awoke with that familiar sense of dread and regret, it felt as though another nail had been banged into the coffin.

Awareness of my alcohol dependency came about like a perfect storm. I finally abandoned my preconceptions of what an alcoholic was, coming to the realisation that to lose control of one's drinking occurs on a sliding scale – you can be weakening in the fight against alcohol a long time before your life hits the skids for good.

I chose to end my fight with booze at the age of thirty-five. I was hurtling along a one-way road to somewhere very unpleasant, and things were only going to get worse. Age impacts on us in many ways, but a noticeable phenomenon that I became aware of following my thirtieth birthday was that I suddenly acknowledged my own mortality. For the first time ever, I actually accepted the fact that yes, one day I would die. I stopped believing that I was going to live for ever, and the drinking and smoking and other bad lifestyle choices became problematic for me. I could no longer bury my head in the sand and ignore the risks – early onset dementia, breast cancer and a plethora of other health consequences loomed on my horizon, and I was scared.

Of course, because of the society in which we live, it can be enormously difficult to perceive one's own drinking habit as being problematic, even if it is. To develop an awareness of this, it's essential that you allow yourself to be guided by your own gut feelings. Nobody else will know how wretched alcohol makes you feel the mornings after, when you're filled with regret for something you did the previous night; nobody will have a clue how much of your thinking time alcohol occupies – the planning, the worrying, the controlling; no one will appreciate just how little self-respect you have because of your drinking habits.

Fully accepting that you cannot control alcohol, whether you are an alcoholic or not, is something only you can do. It's vital that you allow your own feelings on the matter to come to the fore; do not let yourself be bullied by others who might want you to continue drinking because it benefits their own agenda.

In a nutshell, these are the factors that helped me come to the conclusion, finally, that I needed to quit drinking permanently:

- As soon as I opened a bottle of wine, I immediately began to worry about it running out;

- I didn't enjoy my evenings unless drinking alcohol was on the cards;

- I regularly blacked out and lost all memory of the night before;

- I was frightened (as a direct result of the amount of alcohol I was consuming) of developing cancer or liver disease;

- I was ashamed of the way I acted when drunk;

- I was fearful that I could no longer hide my drinking from my daughter and didn't want it to impact negatively on her;

- I stopped convincing myself that the odd positive experience when drinking mitigated the many negative ones;

- I stopped waiting for further proof that I was an alcoholic and just decided that my drinking was sufficiently bad for me to warrant stopping.

And, alongside accepting all of the above, I distanced myself from the commonly held perception of alcohol within western culture: that drinking is a positive and glamorous activity. I gave myself permission to sidestep the norm, to think that maybe alcohol wasn't all it was frequently cracked up to be. I started to question the pros of booze and seriously ponder the cons.

B

Balls to What Anyone Else Thinks

Once you've accepted that you wish to stop drinking altogether and begin to put that into practice, you may discover that family members, your partner and/or friends fail to grasp just how difficult and unmanageable your relationship with alcohol has become. And potentially, an announcement of your impending sobriety will make them feel uneasy for a number of reasons.

First of all, they know they will be losing their boozing partner. If, like me, you utilised alcohol to give you the confidence to morph into the archetypal social butterfly, then without it you will be a different person – a quieter one; someone who is nowhere near as brash and excitable. And if your friendships and relationships have all been born out of the booze-induced version of you, the meaningful others in your life won't have a clue about what you'll become without alcohol buoying you up. And, most likely, that fact will worry them.

As drinkers, and especially as heavy drinkers, we tend to gravitate towards other people who consume lots of alcohol on a regular basis. Partly, this is because of the culture in which we live, with societies in the UK, and the western hemisphere in general, being known for their alcocentric approach to life. Socialising usually revolves around drinking, and we are subjected to countless references within popular culture that reinforce the notion that excessive drinking is completely normal, trivial and virtually expected of us. Over time, we become desensitised to the concept of consuming a mind-altering drug (which is exactly what alcohol is) merely to be sociable. And for people like me, who have trouble stopping when they've had enough, it becomes all too easy to slide, almost unwittingly, into a world of frequent heavy drinking.

A major part of alcohol dependency is denial – it is often described as the only condition where the sufferer is the single person unaware of having it. Commonly what happens is that we gradually surround ourselves with friends who also drink too much because this detracts from our own problem, simultaneously helping us confirm that we don't have an issue with alcohol, thank you very much. We are just doing what everyone else does: having a good time while drinking.

It's a safe little haven, the social world filled with other drinkers, because nobody pulls you up on how pissed you are, or the fact that you were pissed just a couple of days ago and now you're heading that way again, or that you have clapped loads of weight on and look terrible because of the amount of alcohol you are drinking. Why would they? They are all happily in denial of the harms of drinking too much, and if they highlight the negative repercussions it's having on *your* life then it might shine a light on their own habits.

Similarly, it's a fair bet that, if you're part of a couple, your significant other is a drinker, too. Of course, this isn't always the case, especially in circumstances where you've ramped up your consumption later on in life, and you may be in a relationship with a person who can take or leave alcohol. But for many people who are serial binge-drinkers, their social life (which has always been comprised of serial binge-drinking) will probably have led them to meeting their partner, who will be – you've guessed it – a serial binge-drinker.

As I write this I am forty years old and have had one – yes, one – relationship that was not formed while I (or he) was heavily under the influence of alcohol. Unsurprisingly, I met this partner after I had stopped drinking for good, several years into my sobriety. Is this a miraculous coincidence? No, it is not. It's entirely to be expected.

Firstly, a person who does not drink vast amounts of alcohol would have been about as attractive to the boozing me as a worm. I detested it when friends acted sensibly and declared their intentions to have just one or two drinks on a night out because of work, or taking the kids to football the following morning, or any other perfectly legitimate reason for not getting as pissed as a newt. Their opting out of a night of hedonism impinged upon my own freedom to get drunk, for how can two people maintain any kind of conversation when one is sober and the other falling over because they are so inebriated? And this unwillingness of mine to tolerate other people's rightful desires to drink responsibly stretched to boyfriends, too.

I doubt that any of my past partners would have found me in the slightest bit attractive anyway had they been non-drinkers and first met me on a night out, when I was usually loud, obnoxious, slightly wobbly on my legs, flirtatious and quite probably a little bit frightening to anyone who didn't know me.

Assuming that you do have a partner and that person also likes a drink (or ten) then this is more than likely going to cause some issues in your efforts to become alcohol-free. First of all, when you cut out the booze, your social life alters. For me, this was (initially) a fairly drastic recalibration as I virtually stopped going out altogether for several months. I was wary of being around people drinking to get drunk, and I found those who were inebriated to be rather boring once I was permanently sober. And so I became a bit of a hermit.

This tends not to go down well with a partner who enjoys a busy social life, most of it involving alcohol. One of the things that has become blindingly obvious to me since launching Soberistas.com is that people don't like having their alcohol consumption called into question if they don't perceive themselves to have a drink problem. Even when they are downing way more booze than is good for them, if they don't *recognise* their habit as being hazardous then they aren't going to take kindly to people voicing concerns about the harms of drinking too much.

But this quest you are setting out on is not about anyone else. Right at the start of your alcohol-free journey, the only person you should be getting sober for is *you*. And it's vital that you don't waiver on that for anyone else, not even your beloved other half who is maybe a little down in the mouth at losing his or her best drinking buddy. Treat this step as the first tutorial in 'How Not to People Please'. Get selfish (but selfish in a good way – we'll come to this in a minute). People who have low self-esteem, and (in my experience) those who drink to excess, are often guilty of being colossal people pleasers. I've done it. You've probably done it. Perhaps the fact that we put aside our own happiness so much in an effort to placate people and be liked is partly to blame for why we routinely get so pissed.

But here's where that ends. Quitting alcohol has taught me many things about how to live life in a more rewarding way, and one of the biggest lessons has been in learning to follow my own heart. To misquote Frank Sinatra, we should all 'Do it Our Way', because at the end of the day, we can only find true contentment and happiness if we live the life that we, as individuals, feel we should be living.

Telling your partner or friends that you will no longer be partaking in the heavy drinking sessions, a part of your lives for so long, is never going to be a breeze. But here a few pointers for when you reach that monumental moment and announce to your loved ones that you are now a non-drinker:

- Remember that we live in the Land of the Boozers. Your stance as a non-drinker will likely be met with derision, surprise, apathy, disappointment, laughter, confusion or happiness (delete where appropriate). The reaction you receive will depend upon whom you are informing of your decision to become a Soberista, and also upon their relationship with alcohol. Be prepared for all of the above reactions and think ahead as to how you will respond to each.

- You will perhaps have shared with your closest friends or partner your occasional fears regarding the amount you drink and the consequences of your binge-drinking, but maybe not to the full extent that you have experienced those feelings. So when you announce your newfound commitment to sobriety, don't be surprised if people think you are overreacting. What they might perceive as very rare incidents of going over the top are most probably, to you, deeply humiliating and shameful episodes that you feel strongly about never repeating.

  It's unlikely that other people will truly grasp the extent of how wretched your relationship with alcohol has caused you to feel, so don't be swayed by their encouragement to 'just have one', 'loosen up a bit' or 'not be so hard on yourself'. Listen to your own wisdom on this; trust your instincts.

- You may feel tempted to tell a little white lie in the early days and explain your abstinence as being due to a course of antibiotics or the need to drive. This may help in the short term, but you can only rely on these types of explanations temporarily as at some point it will become obvious that you are alcohol-free on a permanent basis. Most people will soon lose interest in the fact that you no longer drink alcohol, and although you may have to deal with a few questions initially, I think it's best to get these out of the way and let the news morph into old news as quickly as possible. As the old adage goes: 'those who matter don't mind and those who mind don't matter'.

- There is no need to declare yourself as an alcoholic when you reveal your new healthy lifestyle choice. Here's what I say to people who quiz me on why I no longer drink: 'I got sick of drinking more than I meant to. I was getting drunk too frequently and I wanted more out of my life than hangovers and feeling like shit.' Done. Walk away. Who cares? It's your life, nobody else's.

When everyone in your immediate circle drinks too much, it's all too simple to fall into a safe world of denial. After all, if he/she is getting sloshed every weekend on prosecco or vodka tonics, it must be OK, right? Because he/she isn't an alcoholic, ergo neither are you. What happens when you step aside from this mass sticking of heads in the sand is that you force the people around you to question their own relationships with alcohol. And, for many, this is intensely uncomfortable and something they would rather not focus on too sharply. An easy way to deflect the attention away from their own boozing is to chastise you for your choice to no longer drink.

Choosing to be alcohol-free in a society that places drinking at the heart of its very essence is a brave and bold thing to do. Essentially, what you are doing is going out on a limb to save yourself, mentally and physically, from the very real harms of excessive alcohol consumption. You will hear the same old rubbish from certain drinkers pertaining to the Nanny State and nobody having the right to tell them not to drink. Whenever I am subjected to this kind of reaction, I remind myself that I have never, and would never, attempt to instruct other people to quit drinking, but that I choose not to drink because I was placing myself in increasingly dangerous situations every time I picked up a glass.

A declaration of sobriety is not relevant to the people who can successfully limit their intake to one or two drinks before calling it a night. I am not one of those people and I doubt you are either, because you are reading this book. If you can't stop drinking once you begin, if you never know when you are drunk, if you have blackouts as a result of drinking more than you set out to, then alcohol is a dangerous substance for you. And you deserve to live a life safe from the negative repercussions it brings about when you consume it.

The generally accepted norm is that alcohol is fun and glamorous, a social lubricant. This positive face of alcohol is one that most out-of-control drinkers wish was applicable to them, but the fact of the matter is it isn't. When friends or family attempt to persuade you to have a little drink with them, they perceive alcohol to be that positive experience and they want you to be able to do the same. But (and this is the crux of the whole issue) alcohol is a different animal for you and me. They are not talking about the same substance, and they will not be able to understand why you can't moderate your consumption and drink responsibly.

This is why stopping drinking, especially when you are part of an alcohol-fuelled social circle, has to be solely about you. I had very low self-esteem and didn't think I was worth a great deal at all when I first put down the bottle. Therefore it was inordinately challenging to put my own needs first by choosing to end the fight with alcohol I'd been engaged in for years. It took a lot of faith, placing my belief firmly in something that I couldn't see or even imagine – a happier life in which I became confident and valued myself again. That transformation did arise eventually, but I had to do a lot óf trusting and waiting first. And the thing I fundamentally trusted was my decision to stop drinking.

'Balls to what anyone else thinks' has to become your motto as you embark on your new life without alcohol. Do whatever it takes to stay sober in the early days, whether that's shirking all social invitations until you feel better able to cope with watching other people drinking, forking out on a posh weekend spa trip, eating too much chocolate and slobbing around the house in a tracksuit or just lying in bed. It doesn't matter! Being a non-drinker takes some adjustment, and as alcohol is everywhere in our society, the first few days or weeks may involve you engaging in a degree of hibernation. So be it. You'll develop confidence and will naturally feel more inclined to get out socially as time goes on, so allow yourself to indulge in whatever you desire if you think it will help keep you off the sauce (as long as it's safe and not illegal or harmful in any other way).

Explain to loved ones that you can't go on putting yourself through the emotional ups and downs that drinking creates in your life, and that you feel you aren't fully in control of your consumption. Plan to do some nice things with your partner or friends that don't feature alcohol as soon as you feel up to it. Be kind to yourself. Remember that this will be the hardest but best decision you will ever take – once you've cracked this non-drinking thing, you'll be able to handle anything. Embrace the challenge, get all the help you need, but, most importantly, *do it for you*!

C

Compassion for Yourself and Everyone Else

How the hell do you learn to be kind to yourself when you've spent years putting yourself down? When you are so well versed in beating yourself up that it has become second nature? When weeks can pass by without you so much as thinking one fleeting positive thought about yourself?

Being unable to control our alcohol intake almost inevitably leads to feelings of self-loathing. There are many reasons for this. For starters, as drinkers we often set ourselves limitations on how much alcohol we will allow ourselves to consume. When we fail to stick to these self-imposed rules we regard ourselves with contempt, 'Why can't you just drink normally like everyone else?' and 'Why did you make such an arse of yourself, again?' being familiar questions rotating around our minds on a loop. And, maddeningly, there are no satisfactory answers. That's just how we are.

Secondly, chances are that if you regularly get smashed on alcohol, then you will say or do things

21

that cause you untold shame and remorse when you wake in the morning with the mother of all hangovers. Dancing on tables and falling over were the least of my worries as a regretful drinker – I frequently acted in ways that made my toes curl the next day, and I let myself and other people down far more often than I care to remember. It's inordinately difficult to laugh such incidents off, particularly as you grow older. Personally, I could just about convince myself that behaving like a drunken idiot was fine when I was twenty; by the time I reached my early thirties it was a different matter entirely.

Thirdly, let's return to the fact that we live in a very boozy society. All around us we see people laughing and having fun with alcohol, and we are taught from an early age that this is what everybody does. As adults, we are told we should be able to work hard but play hard; let off steam with a few drinks at the end of a tough week; look a little bit sexy with tousled hair and a dewy complexion as we dance uninhibitedly with our partner in a smoky nightclub. This is the standard. However, when we slowly lose our ability to control our consumption of alcohol and the sexy moves on the dance floor turn into staggering and falling over, and the drinks with friends morph into being poured into a taxi semi-conscious because we've overdone it, we inadvertently step outside of normal. Because being an alcoholic is such a stigmatised phenomenon in the West, to become the person who cannot control her or his drinking is to feel the cold hand of shame, and that can be a hugely isolating experience.

In addition, it is often the case that people who drink too much initially begin doing so because they possess low self-esteem and are lacking in confidence. Alcohol is brilliant for buoying us up and loosening the tongue in social situations, when ordinarily we may feel restrained by shyness and awkwardness. Therefore, even without any of the above, very concrete, reasons why we dislike ourselves as drinkers, we have commonly started from a staggeringly low point in terms of liking ourselves.

Herein lies a problem. If you have spent virtually your whole adult life not being especially kind to yourself, how on earth do you turn that around in order to start treating yourself with compassion?

The Dalai Lama said, 'If you don't love yourself, you cannot love others. You will not be able to love others. If you have no compassion for yourself then you are not capable of developing compassion for others.' This statement should be employed as the foundation of learning how to exercise self-compassion. Often, we find it easy to be kinder towards others than towards ourselves. It can motivate us to treat ourselves with compassion if we believe we are doing so in order to be kinder to the people we care about. And once self-compassion becomes more engrained in our lives, we will recognise the value in both it and in ourselves.

To begin with, stop regarding yourself as *you*: that person locked inside from whom you want to escape, but can't. Instead, view yourself as *another* – a friend or, better still, you but as a child. When you launch into the internal put-downs and find yourself getting stuck into yet another personal attack, stop, step back and observe. Would you ever stand by and watch someone talking in this way to a friend? Or, if you could travel back in time, would you do nothing to help yourself as a child if an angry and unreasonable grown-up was shouting you down?

Human beings are all fallible. We make mistakes; we drift into unhelpful and destructive patterns of behaviour; we let people down; we shout; we are, on occasion, unable to manage our emotions successfully. As we travel along the journeys of our lives, we learn from all of these things and grow as people. This is what life is: a series of lessons, and we should regard ourselves as one of our best teachers. When a child does something silly, an act that stems from their naïvety, most adults do not become cross and shout. It is a far more usual response to try and educate the child to help them understand what went wrong and show them how better to go about things the next time. This is compassion. It is understanding. It is kindness.

There is nothing inhuman about getting things wrong – in fact, quite the opposite. It would be bizarre and totally abnormal if we made it through our entire lives without ever putting a foot wrong. To make mistakes is to be human. And yet, when it comes to us as individuals, we frequently chastise ourselves for acting stupidly or because we've done something we wish we hadn't.

A few years into my sobriety I started to accept all that I was as an animal, how many of my characteristics are fixed as a result of my genetic composition, and how youth and emotional immaturity have a lot to answer for when it comes to the mistakes of the past. We as humans are brilliant at adaptation – at learning habits and behaviours. Our brains are forever being moulded as the neurological pathways are reinforced repeatedly by the things we do. There is much evidence pointing towards us having no free will at all, and while this should not be taken as carte blanche to act however we please (because we *can* learn to do things differently if we stick with a new habit for long enough), it can be utilised as a way to be a little less harsh on ourselves.

In an article posted on psychologytoday.com entitled 'Do We Have Free Will?' Seth Schwartz PhD explains:

There is no consensus within psychology as to whether we really do have free will – although much of our field seems to assume that we don't. Freud and Skinner didn't agree on very much, but one thing they did agree on was that human behavior was determined by influences within or outside the person. Freud talked about unconscious conflicts as causes of behavior, and Skinner talked about environmental contingencies, but either way we were not free to decide.

Much of modern-day life seems to suggest the opposite: that we *are* making our own choices all of the time and we have complete control over every aspect of day-to-day living, but much of the science surrounding this area indicates this is not the case. We are driven by many factors, and certainly, when one acknowledges the addictive nature of alcohol, we are not acting as free agents when under the influence of this substance.

Let's remember that alcohol is an addictive drug; millions are spent on its marketing and advertising each year, and it is widely and cheaply available. As a lesson in self-compassion, I found it enormously helpful to educate myself about the alcohol industry, its power and how manipulative it is in terms of affecting society's attitudes. In doing so, I wasn't letting myself off the hook, but appreciating just how much of an unwitting pawn I'd been in the wide scale game played by the alcohol industry giants: creating a need while simultaneously proposing that responsible drinkers do not *need* to drink, they *choose* to drink.

A 2015 report by the Organisation for Economic Co-operation and Development (OECD) entitled 'Tackling Harmful Alcohol Use' revealed that dangerous drinking among better-educated women had contributed to an upward trend in alcohol consumption in the UK during a thirty-year period. Those of us who fall foul of the normalisation of everyday drinking in substantial quantities are generally not stupid. We know the risks and yet we go on for years, dipping in and out of denial – moments of clarity regarding the health harms to which we are subjecting our bodies, followed by buying into slapdash caution-to-the-wind sayings such as 'one for the road' or 'I've got to die of something'.

There is more going on than choice when it comes to out-of-control drinking. Some of us may be able to sail through life, getting drunk whenever we fancy it, and never feeling the harsh slap of that special brand of self-hatred that comes from losing the fight with alcohol. But the millions of people who gradually become dependent drinkers don't get away that easily. As a result of our genes, the ways in which we've been socialised and our physiology, we can find ourselves in a state of complete despair because of the bottle. And, crucially, we are not alone.

At the time of writing, 10.8m adults in the UK drink at levels that are harmful to their health (Alcohol Concern). And research conducted by the University of Southampton published in January 2016 (using data from the National Health Survey for England) revealed that the alcohol industry's main source of profits are derived from 'hazardous' and 'harmful' drinkers. The former group made up thirty-eight per cent of total sales of alcoholic drinks, while harmful drinkers made up thirty-one per cent. And so the myth that responsible drinkers are the norm, and those of us drinking more than we should represent a tiny minority of irresponsible drinkers who, quite frankly, should be ashamed of ourselves, is nonsense. The UK is awash with heavy drinkers, and the alcohol industry plays on this fact and benefits financially from it in a major way.

When I drank, I was rather selfish. I think drinking too much on a regular basis makes you that way. Because alcohol is an addictive substance, over time people become reliant on it, either psychologically or physically, and when that happens, the booze takes precedence over most other things. Certainly in my own case, drinking took priority over worries about my health, or the need to be more emotionally present for my daughter, or financial concerns, or any element of living that didn't involve the consumption of alcohol.

Conversely, however, I never regarded myself as selfish, because in my mind selfish people were overly confident, and I was definitely not that. But looking back, I can see that narcissism – inordinate fascination with oneself – played a substantial part in my drink-related misery. I was deeply immersed in a small existence, one that focused acutely on *me* – what other people thought of me; how other people reacted to me; how I was treated. I did not have a grasp on taking responsibility for my actions, and much of the time I acted like a petulant teenager in the face of accusations. Nothing was ever my fault, I absolutely could not empathise, and most of the time my own needs and desires came ahead of everyone else's.

Despite being primarily concerned with myself, I was not exercising compassion. I label this phenomenon 'negative narcissism', and it prevented me from loving myself. I was wrapped up in a state of bitterness, thinking the world was out to get me and the only thing that I could call a true friend came in the shape of a bottle.

True love for oneself is not narcissism; it is not

selfish. It stems, first of all, from allowing yourself to get to know who you are, minus the mind-altering properties of alcohol. If you are able to recognise your flaws and your greatest qualities, your uniqueness and your character in all its facets, *and* you can accept yourself for being all that you are, only *then* are you exercising self-compassion. But when alcohol comes top of your priorities, it is impossible to develop the type of emotional maturity that enables this level of self-awareness to occur.

An excellent motivator in quitting drinking is to accept that simply by removing alcohol from your life, you are allowing yourself the opportunity to develop emotionally, and eventually this will lead to self-compassion. Not drinking is the first step in being kind to yourself, because when you weigh up the pros and cons of regular and excessive consumption, you'll see that it undermines you on a fairly consistent basis. In the initial period of being a non-drinker, all you need to do in order to kick-start the habit of being kind to yourself is to remain a non-drinker. If you perceive this to be an opportunity to learn a new way, to uncover a more fulfilling life, it becomes less about missing out and far more about moving into an exciting new chapter of your life – one in which you actually get to know yourself for the first time as an adult.

When you are weighed down in a world of negative narcissism, it is virtually impossible to form positive, mutually fulfilling relationships. But when you are able to love yourself, compassion for others becomes so much easier, and when you act empathetically towards the people you interact with, their reaction towards you will be more positive. This increasingly favourable response reinforces your self-esteem, and so the virtuous circle turns. Put very simply, when you are compassionate towards yourself, you are able to be compassionate towards other people. Which brings us back to what the Dalai Lama said:

If you don't love yourself, you cannot love others. You will not be able to love others. If you have no compassion for yourself then you are not capable of developing compassion for others.

From a starting block of self-hatred, it is very difficult to imagine ever loving yourself. But the only thing you need to do right at the beginning of your alcohol-free journey is not drink. That's it. The rest will follow naturally. In addition, it certainly won't hurt to introduce activities into your daily life that make you feel good about yourself – a warm candlelit bath with beautiful scented oils; an hour sitting in the garden with the sun shining down and a good book or your favourite magazine to read; indulging in some of your favourite foods (although a good tip initially is to avoid anything that might trigger a craving – pasta, for instance, always made me lust after red wine in the early days of not drinking); having a massage or beauty treatment.

If you aren't used to pampering yourself then it may feel alien in the beginning, but treating yourself to pleasant experiences is a helpful way to reinforce that you are worth being nice to, and it's also a useful way to distract yourself from thinking about drinking. Over time, the requirement to battle cravings won't be anywhere near so prevalent and you'll grow accustomed to being good to yourself, so any awkwardness will disappear. Every day that you don't drink, you will be allowing yourself to get to know the person inside – the perfect imperfections, the bits that make you proud of yourself and the characteristics that are so uniquely yours. And, slowly, you will learn to like yourself again.

D

Downtime Is Important

Waking up at first light, diving out of bed, straight under the shower, helping children to get ready for school, slapping on some make-up in record time, pulling a brush through our hair – how many of us begin our day in this way? Before it's even 8 a.m. we have probably achieved more than we did as teenagers in an entire day. And then we have a full eight hours at work to get through, followed by dinner to prepare and any housework that needs doing, which we cram into the short evening hours before collapsing into bed, exhausted. And then we repeat the whole thing again the next day, and the next. And weekends – when did they stop equating to two rest days? Oh yes, it was when we grew up and suddenly found ourselves with responsibilities larger than bringing our PE bag home for the wash on a Friday after school.

Alcohol is frequently considered to be a fast-track vehicle for unwinding, an easy treat which aids the transition between the manic daytime and relaxing night time, and this notion of drinking as a relaxant substantially helps the alcohol industry to accrue its profits. We live in a cash-rich and time-poor society, so who has the spare hours necessary to seek a sublime, serene state of mind by means other than the obvious – a cold (supersized) glass of Chardonnay? Messages abound within popular culture that women especially deserve a big glass of wine in the evening, and this is what all busy mums are doing in order to chill out after the kids have been safely tucked in bed. And there's no doubt about it: supping on that vino definitely helps put the brakes on doing anything else.

However, the imagery depicting alcohol consumption that we are subjected to via the alcohol industry's advertisements never portrays the darker side of drinking. We are not shown the drunken woman, slumped on the settee semi-conscious with mascara streaked across her cheeks; we do not see the couple arguing loudly after a few bottles, shouting and bawling over a trivial matter that would never have come to the fore had it not been for alcohol's involvement; we are not privy to the hungover parent who snaps at their child for no reason other than being sleep-deprived.

We return to the fact that as problem drinkers (and by this I mean people who have no off-switch, who drink habitually and whose lives are frequently and negatively affected by their alcohol consumption), we are not featured in the preferred societal vision of what drinking is all about. What we see in the advertising and marketing of alcohol products is not what we experience when we drink. And so the glass-of-wine-to-relax-at-the-end-of-a-busy-day never works out that way. It becomes a bottle, sometimes two. And those bottles become the source of another truckload of problems to deal with the following day. Those bottles further damage our self-esteem and cause us to hate ourselves again for what we did or didn't do as a result of drinking too much.

What we may believe (and who can blame us when one considers the extent of the positive messages surrounding alcohol consumption in the West?) to be a pleasant and innocuous means of relaxation is, for problem drinkers, a fast-track route to more misery. And it's a great way to add to the chaos of our lives, because drinking erodes hours of the day that could be used for getting organised and achieving proper rest.

Reality check firmly in place (for people who cannot moderate their alcohol intake) and it's clear that booze is not particularly effective for attaining true relaxation. Viewed over the entirety of a week, as opposed to just the short burst of perceived mental decompression that we feel after the first glass, alcohol adds to our burden of stress and simultaneously decreases the number of available hours we have outside of work and sleep. This in turn heightens the intensity of our busy lives, leaving us with even less time to get things done.

Here then is a fantastic outcome of becoming a non-drinker: several hours are reclaimed in the name of booze-free evenings. Rather than slumping in front of the television, slowly transforming into a comatose vegetable, you will discover that all those chores (supermarket shopping, ironing, sorting bills out, organising school administration for the kids, tidying up, etc.), once considered irritants due to the fact that they got in the way of drinking, are easily completed. This, happily, creates free time – time to do things that bring you pleasure; time to relax properly; time to be creative; time to feel good about yourself. Downtime.

When I drank alcohol, I thought people with hobbies were slightly dull. I was consistently seeking elevation from the humdrum, a route out of the boring minutiae of everyday life, and drinking was my preferred means of achieving this aim. Yes, hobbies amounted to a distraction from boredom, which was precisely why I drank, but in my deluded mind drinking appeared to be a worthwhile exercise, whereas collecting stamps or trainspotting did not. And so I steered clear of pursuing any pastimes for no other reason than they would interfere with my boozing. If I had a free afternoon at the weekend I wanted to be in the pub, not sitting at home arranging stamps.

When I first quit drinking I had a real problem with sitting still. I had absolutely no idea how to just be: to spend time alone, sober, relaxed and untroubled. The discomfort of being that way was almost physical; my skin itched and my limbs felt restless, and I was powerless to reach a state of serenity without a drink to calm me down. Or so I thought. But over time, as with anything, the sensation of being sober and calm, clear-headed and happy to be me, unfettered by any stresses or anxieties, became the norm.

I've always loved music, but when I first became a non-drinker I found that many of the albums I'd loved triggered cravings. Accordingly, I stopped listening to them. I entered a void that lasted for several months –a barren life that featured little else but the basics: sleeping, eating and looking after my daughter, the dog and the house. I found it impossible to engage in anything that I had done in my past life, the drinking one, because it all seemed to be pointless without alcohol. At the time I was aware of this, and recognised it as being really rather sad that a life can only have significance if alcohol is a part of it.

And so I set about putting things right.

My downtime became, among other interests, about listening to music – old favourites and new stuff. I even started going to gigs again, an experience that had always been especially alcohol-fuelled. Gradually, the associations with drinking disappeared and music was reinstated as a big priority. I realised how happy music makes me, what a hugely important role it plays in my life. And without alcohol slowing me down and keeping me trapped in the same repetitive cycles, I've begun to listen to a wider range of artists, paying more attention to each one than I ever used to when drunk.

Over the last few alcohol-free years, I've incrementally tuned out the elements of my life that caused me stress and made me feel uninspired, and have increased the component parts that fill me with happiness and make me feel alive. Downtime, the hours I spend outside of work and essential jobs, is vital for keeping me mentally grounded and in tune with the person I am. As I have finally found it possible to exercise self-compassion, I've naturally allowed myself to indulge in all the things I enjoy: music, running, writing, hiking, travelling. And the more I fill my time with activities that I love so much, the less space there is for the crap – the endless efforts of big business to push on to us their ideas and lifestyle aspirations.

I grew up believing that if you were cool, you drank, and if you were boring, you did not. A very black and white state of affairs; a notion that was born out of alcohol marketing and advertisements and which had little to do with the truth. Not drinking does not equate to being dull. I know for a fact that as a non-drinker, I am a million times more interesting than the person who drank her nights away repeatedly, stuck in a cycle of inebriation and hungover depression.

With a cluttered, alcohol-fogged headspace, my life was complicated by a myriad of troubles, some real and some not. Every single thought that passed through my mind I considered to be valid, worth paying attention to. When I look back on the way I lived, my cognitive processes represented a jumbled melee of problems and twisted logic, making me feel as if, mentally, I was fighting my way out of a thick bramble patch every day. I utilised alcohol as a way to achieve temporary respite from the confusion, but ultimately it only served to add to the clouding of my mind.

Being sober all the time has taught me that the

simpler an existence we live, the happier we are. By simple I don't mean that we do nothing with our free time; instead, it's about learning what makes us tick, acknowledging our likes and dislikes and doing more of the former and less of the latter.

Modern society is built upon a complex labyrinth of messages all persuading us to do this and that, the majority of them being powered by capitalism and consumerism. With a lack of awareness, it's easy to be swept along by the persuasive techniques of the media, believing that looking a certain way will bring us happiness, or wearing a particular pair of jeans will make us more attractive. And all of these messages combine to fill our headspace with clutter: pointless and wasteful thoughts that provide us with nothing but a loss of our freedom. Simplifying our existences by creating blinkers that shut these influences out provides us with the room to be ourselves, untethered and able to choose a life that suits us as individuals.

The definition of 'downtime' in the 1999 Concise Oxford English Dictionary is as follows: 'time during which a computer or other machine is out of action'. There is no mention of the word relating to human beings, although more recent definitions now include such a reference: 'Downtime for a person is a time when the person can relax' (Cambridge Dictionaries Online). Often it feels as though we *are* machines, with life rattling along while we meekly obey orders to keep all the plates spinning. And the endless tidal wave of consumerist values and empty promises helps create the illusion that we must keep going –

the road to success is everything and we do not have the luxury of stepping off. The fact that downtime has, only in more recent years, come to denote a person's demarcation from working time, as opposed to referring solely to a machine being out of action, suggests that this phenomenon has crept up in significance. Busier lives and heightened stress levels have resulted in more people finding it essential to draw a line between working and not in order to squeeze in at least a few hours where they are free from demands.

Downtime isn't a luxury, it's a requirement. When we are able to create a space where we can be at one with the world, where nobody is on our backs to produce a report, or get the ironing done, or book a table at a restaurant, or take the dog out, or wash the pots, or drive somebody somewhere, or change a bed, or vacuum the house, or make us feel terrible for not being a size 10, or do *anything* that detracts from simply being, we are preserving ourselves. Rushing around like headless chickens, always catering for the needs of others, putting pressure on ourselves to be perfect and never indulging in me time is a sure fire way to fuel the urge to drink in order to bring about a release from the internal compression.

As I have grown older, and definitely as I have spent longer living without alcohol, I have increasingly recognised the need to escape. It's always a brief and temporary respite, but I happily bail out of the rat race on a fairly regular basis, and I advise you to do the same. Some people will employ alcohol to flee the demands of the modern world, but, as we covered earlier on in this chapter, if you cannot control your alcohol intake then opting to drink is certain to create tension rather than resolving it.

Try things, spend time alone and figure out what it is that you enjoy doing. And then do it. It sounds simple because it is. I love going away for a couple of days to somewhere in the middle of nowhere as it affords me time and space away – not from just the busyness of my everyday life, but also the endless bombardment of the consumerist messages that we are all subjected to. The more remote the places that I reach, the better, and when I return home I am guaranteed to feel relaxed and able to pick up where I left off with ten times the energy and optimism that I had prior to my departure.

But even when you're staying put at home, it's crucial to fit in some downtime. If you need to shoo the kids off somewhere for a few hours, then do so – lock the bathroom door and stick your headphones in, or go for a run or a walk where nobody will be able to bother you. Downtime is about clearing your mind and obtaining a purely relaxed state of being. How you achieve that is a completely personal matter – it might be a yoga class; a knitting group; reading a book; lying on the floor staring at the ceiling; gardening. Whatever works best for you, just do it. And view your downtime as a key component in staying happy and focusing on being alcohol-free.

Drinking does not equal downtime for people who cannot moderate their alcohol intake. It might offer us a fantasy world where the wheels of the daily grind are brought to a halt temporarily, but it is exactly that: a fantasy. However, that need to escape once in a while does not evaporate merely because you have become alcohol-free; if anything, it increases. Carve out downtime hours from every week, and treat them as sacrosanct. If you intend to keep alcohol out of your life for good, this is precisely what they are.

E

Engage With Other People Who Know How You Feel

Human beings are tribal. The desire to belong to a group is apparent when we observe football fans, crowds at music gigs or children waiting to be picked for a sports team at school. While it's good to feel comfortable in one's uniqueness, it's undeniable that we all want to feel accepted at some level, even if only by a single other.

Possessing an inability to control the amount of alcohol you consume is guaranteed to make you feel divorced from wider society, owing to the fact that drinking is such a normalised activity in the West. Of course, it's perceived by the majority as being perfectly acceptable to drink too much and become ever so slightly squiffy at a Christmas do, birthday party, wedding or when on holiday, but only if you do it very occasionally and without the distinct air of desperation. Should you cross the line and venture into dependency territory then things will probably turn a little bleak.

As we touched upon earlier in this book, at the

point when most people feel charged to put down the bottle permanently, their self-esteem is not usually buoyant. They are often embarking on the alcohol-free road to happiness and contentment with substantial emotional baggage, feeling about as confident as a newborn lamb wobbling about on shaky legs. And, annoyingly, as this is a time when sizeable dollops of self-belief and gumption are called for, alcohol suddenly appears to be a tempting option once again, and around and around the vicious circle spins.

It's a strange dichotomy in the West that although we are brought up imbued with the notion that teamwork is a good thing ('there's no I in team!'), by the time most of us approach adulthood we are frequently of the mind-set that asking for help signifies weakness. Women especially are schooled to believe that we are all fabulous multi-taskers – yes, we *can* have it all, and to be anything less than perfect is to be deeply flawed. It's an embarrassing admission for lots of people when they find themselves unable to control their alcohol intake, and so to ask for help is virtually unthinkable – I got myself into this mess, I'll dig myself out of it. We have a habit of severing mental from physical impairment when it comes to seeking help. It would be utterly out of the question for us to allow a broken leg to worsen at home, alone and with no medical support whatsoever. And yet, for a problem that arises in the mind (not simply addiction, which can be physical too, but also the issues which commonly lend themselves to developing a reliance upon alcohol, such as bereavement, loneliness, divorce and stress), many people will do just that: suffer in silence, ashamed, mortified and too scared to ask for help.

Furthermore, lots of people who are alcohol dependent won't even *know* this to be the case, instead looking to a plethora of alternative reasons behind why they seemingly possess no control whatsoever when it comes to their drinking habits – 'It was just a one-off, I hadn't eaten enough before I hit the wine' or 'I don't normally touch spirits, it was those that did me in.' And so, unlike having a broken leg, it's often easier to plough on with life under the misguided belief that things are simply as they are and there is nothing anyone can do to change them. God forbid it might be the alcohol – and reliance upon it.

For approximately eight years from the age of twenty-seven, I operated in accordance with the miserable conclusion that I had been dealt a bad hand in life – my divorce, followed by a series of rather unsatisfying relationships, jobs that were about as exciting as a wet rag, and a generally gloomy perspective. This, looking back, I realise was definitely alcohol-induced depression, but then it was something I routinely put down to my personality. (I thought I had bipolar disorder for quite some time. Funnily enough, once the alcohol disappeared from my world, so did the wildly fluctuating mood swings.)

One night I went to a party with my then-boyfriend. He was a reasonably big drinker, and our joint social life was heavily bound up in alcohol. This party had warning lights flashing all over it – lights that were so bright I should have picked up on them from miles away. However, in my deeply deluded state of mind as a boozer, I trotted along, unaware of any danger, intent on sticking to my plan of going steady, sipping beer while avoiding wine and spirits, and interspersing my drinks with plenty of water. The likelihood of this actually occurring was, of course, zero. The best laid plans of mice and men, or, in this instance, of a woman with absolutely no confidence when in new company and a rather worrying dependency upon alcohol.

Very quickly, I became extraordinarily drunk, flirting outrageously with all and sundry and adopting my usual persona of loud and irritating, a state which always (and this party was no exception) preceded my passing out mid-conversation. I awoke, fully clothed, upstairs in a spare bedroom at about 5 a.m. The boyfriend had departed (I suspected in a huff), and I had an almighty hangover. Cold fingers of fear rapidly began to work their special magic, infiltrating my paranoid mind with wild fantasies about my behaviour the previous night. It was always especially worrying when my partner was not present, as this led me to conclude that I had acted in a sexually provocative manner with another man right in front of his face (which is, in reality, what regularly happened). I crept downstairs, gathered up my bag and coat, and let myself out of the house silently.

The male host of the party, in discussion with my

boyfriend a couple of days later, had this to say with regard to my exploits:, 'Why can't she just stop when she's had enough?'

And there, my friends, we have it: the acutely obvious, clear-as-daylight you-cannot-ignore-this-fact-because-it's-blatantly-true reason why discovering a tribe of people who know how it feels to be out of control with booze is vital for our sanity. Those who don't feel how we do about alcohol *do not get it*. It's as though they are comprised of different materials. Their brains work in totally opposing ways to those of people who do not have an off-switch. And no matter how hard you try, you're unlikely to be successful in educating them fully as to the ways of the problem drinker.

How can you expect a non-problem drinker to appreciate that, although you set out to imbibe only two or three drinks, maybe four maximum, you did, in fact, consume in excess of three bottles of wine all by yourself? How will they ever wrap their head around the fact that you have no sensation of being drunk, and even when you are falling all over the place and slurring your words, inside you actually consider yourself to be fully with it and looking pretty damn fine? And perhaps the most confusing concept of all, how do you explain that deep within you, each time you go out drinking you are hoping, on that occasion, you will be magically transformed into a responsible drinker – even when all the evidence from years of disastrous episodes involving booze points conclusively to the fact that you cannot moderate your intake? The answer to all of these questions is that you can't, because the very phenomenon of problem drinking is a mad one. It doesn't even make sense to us, the ones who are living with it.

The solution to this quandary is to find those who *do* understand – other people who feel the same way as you do. On a personal level, a surprising side effect of establishing Soberistas.com was that I recognised my *own* need to interact (even if it was done so passively via reading other people's blogs on a daily basis) with fellow problem drinkers. Having knowledge that there are thousands of normal, lovely people spread between all the corners of the world who, like me, have no control over the amount of alcohol they drink once they pick up the first glass has gifted me with an overwhelming sense of togetherness and community. I have never felt alone since the first days of the website's life, and this in itself has been a highly significant element of my own contentment and happiness.

We need to feel as though we belong to a group, that we aren't in some way freakish. And while I acknowledged this fact in the planning phase of Soberistas (indeed, it was this realisation that led me to launching the site in the first place), I neglected to see that I needed to connect with like-minded souls too. Why? Because we all do – we are human beings, after all.

The danger of attempting to quit drinking on a stand-alone basis is that, in addition to dealing with the myriad of new situations and emotions that arise constantly, there's a high probability that you will feel wretched and completely misunderstood – neither state of mind being particularly conducive to building internal resistance and self-esteem. People who have lived through the whole quitting drinking business will be able to offer advice, support and endless sympathetic nods of the head and hand-holding (virtual if online) amid the more challenging scenarios. Knowing you aren't alone is a very simple but effective piece of ammunition in the road to wellness, and there is no easier way to acquire this knowledge than to mingle on one of the many internet resources existing purely for that purpose.

There is another reason why having friends who are in the same boat as you with regard to alcohol is a good idea: people who are in your tribe will never convince you that it's OK to 'just have one'.

About eighteen months after I quit drinking, I was walking with an old friend. Around that time I was casually entertaining fantastical notions of enjoying a few drinks – a 'reward', as I perceived it, for the year and a half I had just spent pregnant and breastfeeding. Having recovered a substantial percentage of my physical independence, the idea of alcohol had once again reared its belligerent head in my mind, and with a reasonable length of sobriety behind me, complacency had begun to set in a little.

'Why can't I go out for a night and let my hair down?' I posed the question to my companion with an air of defiance. His answer, delivered from someone who had not known fully the numerous desperate and tragic events that had arisen from my ongoing wish to 'let my hair down', was exactly what I wanted to hear.

'You can! My God, you've been pregnant for ages and have been living like a hermit. Get yourself out there and go for it!'

Hurrah! Licence to drink. The cogs began to whir immediately as I started laying plans for my long-awaited return to the Land of the Boozers.

And then, a while later, I found myself at home alone, staring out of the window and feeling suddenly glum. The last time I had drunk alcohol I'd run a serious risk of death, either via choking on my own vomit or being attacked/maimed/murdered as I staggered around the dark streets late at night, alone and completely out of it. What had begun as a couple of glasses of Chablis had concluded with the draining of three bottles of wine and a litre of strong cider, and a night of serious self-loathing in my local hospital.

With a sinking heart I reminded myself in no uncertain terms that I couldn't go out and let my hair down without seriously damaging myself, mentally and physically. My vision of laughing and dancing the night away with the at-ease manner of a woman who is very slightly inebriated was, in reality, a load of old tosh. And so, it was with gargantuan willpower and by giving myself a good talking to that I put to rest my momentary whimsical plans of going out and getting pissed.

The internal discussion I endured would have been so much easier to manage had it not been internal at all, but a conversation with an understanding friend – someone who, like me, was utterly unable to have a few drinks before calling it a night safely. Belonging to a tribe of people, no matter how big or small, who can remind you in a timely and non-patronising manner why you should not ever touch alcohol is not merely sensible, but crucial in my view. It takes just one moment of weakness, if you are relying on willpower alone to stay strong in the face of overwhelmingly convincing murmurings from the Wine Witch, and all could be lost. With backup in the shape of a group of friends who totally understand and know how you feel, life becomes so much easier to navigate.

The same as in every other area of our lives, we want to belong to someone, to feel accepted and loved despite our flaws – or, as I prefer to see them, our perfect imperfections.

F

Feel, Deal, Heal

Riddle: when is a feeling not a feeling?
Answer: when you're pissed.

When I was newly divorced I spent a few weeks
visiting a counsellor who speedily deduced that my
emotional maturity had frozen at around the age of
fifteen. Funnily enough, this was the exact point at
which I launched into an enthusiastic love affair with
the bottle, and from then onwards any emotion that
wafted my way was swiftly put in its place by a few
drinks.

In my early thirties, it came as something of a
revelation to me that I was not considered to be an
emotionally aware individual. This is remarkable
now, when I think back to the person I was as a
boozer, because I possessed literally no reserves
when it came to internal wisdom, and my reactions
were consistently kneejerk. I had zero understanding
of how our thoughts don't *actually* have to be taken
notice of: we can allow them to drift through our
minds like clouds in a beautiful blue sky, selecting
only those to which we choose to pay attention.

Conversely, I would jump onto every whim, cling to each impulse, all the while not knowing who I was or how I should be living.

And then I quit drinking. And Oh. My. God. Did those emotions hit like a tsunami? (Yes, they did, although that was a rhetorical question.) I was totally unprepared for this sledgehammer-like onslaught of feelings, especially because so many of them were dredged up from years, if not decades, earlier. The big one came in the shape of my divorce emotions. Upon the demise of my short-lived marriage when I was aged twenty-seven I think I cried once, subsequently smothering the many rivers of unshed tears with bottle after bottle of wine. Thus, upon ditching the booze, I was knocked sideways with sadness, anger and what can only be described as wretchedness whenever that unhappy time sprang to mind (which was frequently to begin with).

As I ventured further along the sober path, I ruminated over the death of my beloved grandparents and my first dog, George. I agonised over the occasions when I had drunk too much to be a responsible and emotionally present parent to my daughter. I relived the instances when, drunk and overwrought, I had seriously considered ending my life. And for a long time, it hurt like hell inside. Most of these tortuous internal breakdowns took place privately without my sharing them with anyone. There were many nights when I spent hours crying myself to sleep, lots of times when I could hardly bear to remain in my own skin, and the only way I could escape the sensation was to run a long way, as fast as I could, until my lungs screamed.

It is unsurprising that the above happened. I had not truly *felt* a feeling for more than twenty years, and those emotions, they don't go away. You cannot dispose of them by consuming alcohol; all the drinking does is to herd your unfelt emotions into a box and close the lid, those feelings quietly waiting for release day. And when they find freedom it's like being submerged in an almighty whirlwind, with every conceivable emotion rising, full of rage and intensity, and bringing you to your knees.

A couple of years after becoming a non-drinker I wrote a blog entitled 'The Four Emotional Stages of Sobriety'. I include it here.

I stopped drinking in April 2011, embarking on a journey that began in the early hours of one spring morning and which has taken me on a convoluted and emotionally turbulent ride, finally allowing me to climb off into somewhere that resembles contentment and emotional stability. For anyone who has recently ditched alcohol, I have written the following, outlining the different emotional stages I travelled through in the twenty-three months between my last drink and today. I hope that it might help those new to sobriety, giving you a bit of a heads up on what to expect in this new and exciting chapter of your life.

Stage 1 – The joys of the natural high

As an alcohol-dependent person who had felt terribly out of control of her own life for many, many years, the first few weeks and months of living as a non-drinker were a breath of fresh air. The joy of waking up each day and not immediately running through a mental checklist of those whom I had insulted/let down/hurt the night before was beyond compare. I literally jumped out of bed each day, a massive weight of anxiety removed from around my neck. Gone were the fears of developing breast cancer or dying of liver failure, the dreaded guilt and shame that I'd suffered as a result of doing something stupid and/or irresponsible when under the influence – I felt free as a bird.

Going out socially was a wonderful experience, as previously I had always felt butterflies in my stomach as I feared how the night would unfold, never knowing how drunk I would get and where that state of mind would take me. Instead I knew that I was finally calling the shots – I would decide whom to talk to, what I said, whether or not I chatted someone up/allowed myself to be chatted up. This was me, and not that idiot who I became after too much wine. This first period was characterised by a sense of freedom, lightness and joy.

Stage 2 – Boredom, and why me?

OK, nothing lasts for ever. After a couple of months, I became beset by a black mood and the doubts began to creep in. The little devil on my shoulder grew in his boldness, and whereas the angel had definitely ruled the roost in the early weeks, the voice of addiction became louder and more assertive in this second phase. These were the type of exchanges I had with my devil:

'What if you aren't addicted to alcohol? What if you just need to learn how to moderate? Could it be that your boyfriend would prefer you to be more under control to suit him better, and that's why he professed concern at how much you were drinking? Who is he to think he can control you? Doesn't he see that you are a free spirit? You don't run with the crowds; you are different, untamed. Alcohol is a part of who you are. Everyone else in the world is allowed to drink and get drunk – why the hell can't you? It's not fair.

In the midst of this period, I initiated a blazing row with my boyfriend and told him in no uncertain terms that I was planning on drinking that night. He tried in vain to convince me that it was the addiction talking, but how could it be? It was so convincing and powerful – that was *me* talking; the voice was coming right from within me. We stormed up to the pub together and he ordered himself a pint and sat outside. I scuttled up to the bar after he had taken his seat, my heart beating ferociously and my cheeks burning.

Every piece of me wanted to buy alcohol except for the tiniest voice, hidden somewhere deep inside me. It told me that I would never change if I bought a glass of wine now; this moment was definitive – it would determine whether I stayed on the path to self-discovery and a better life or returned hell for leather to that old path of destruction. I couldn't let myself down, and I stuck to my guns.

I ordered a lime and soda.

Stage 3 – Resolute but bitter

I turned a corner that night and all doubt was removed. The devil fell away from my shoulder, but nothing replaced him for a long time. There were months in a vacuum; I accepted my lot as a non-drinker, but I wasn't happy about it. I missed alcohol terribly – I wanted to sit outside pubs in the summer, laughing gaily over a big glass of icy cold white wine. I wanted to get glammed up and drink cocktails in a fancy bar, enjoying the sense of relaxation, of throwing caution to the wind and forgetting my cares for a night. At times, I hated other people for being 'allowed' to drink. This was a very difficult stage.

After several months of this, I read Jason Vale's book *How to Kick the Drink ... Easily!*

and my life changed. I saw alcohol for what it really was, and I knew that all the voices and cravings I had felt over the last year or so were the result of slowly weaning myself off a very powerful and prevalent socially-acceptable drug. I gave myself a break, and began to let go of the regrets and shame that I was still carrying around with me. The bitterness slowly dissolved into contentment; the sun began to shine once more.

Stage 4 – Understanding me as a non-drinker

The final stage is the best. Over the last couple of years I have worked through many emotions and feelings of regret, sadness, anger, bitterness, sorrow, remorse, jealousy and fear. After a good year and a half, the negativity noticeably reduced. As my self-esteem grew and my appreciation of the world and everything in it was heightened, due to the clarity that came from not poisoning my body with alcohol on an almost daily basis, it was as though the bad thoughts were mopped up one by one by my new found positivity and optimistic take on life.

I stopped experiencing wine envy when I walked past a pub full to bursting with drunken, loud revellers, but I didn't huff and puff either – drinking is their choice, just as *not drinking* is mine. I love my life and I am grateful every day that alcohol no longer plays a part in it. I never have moments on a Friday night like the ones I had in the early days – DVD, nice bottle of wine, oh how wonderful it would feel to kick back and slowly feel the wine ameliorating all my anxieties. It simply isn't a part of my consciousness any more – I drove it out and replaced my addiction with happiness and good health.

It would have been perhaps easier to jump straight from Stage One to Stage Four, but the journey has allowed me to learn so much about who I really am, minus the veneer of alcohol, and I wouldn't have missed it out even if I could have. I had no idea that when I stopped drinking it would be necessary to undergo such emotional turbulence, feeling as though my old self has been through a seriously intense recalibration before being reinstalled with a new lease of life, eventually leaving a turbocharged version of me back in the driving seat of my life. I didn't expect any of that, but I am 100% happy that it happened.

The process described in this blog post unfolded over the course of two years and was pretty awful during the initial phase. As I perceive it now, there is no short cut to take, no easy way to navigate our way through all the emotional upheaval. It's a process that is absolutely necessary if we are to acquire the tools we'll need to go forward and lead the same life that people who have never struggled with an addiction lead. It boils down to learning to handle our emotions as adults, and it's what most people who drink to excess fail to manage until they get sober.

The outcome of living through such an emotional rollercoaster is that I now feel like a very grounded, well-adjusted human being. My reactions to situations are appropriate, I never feel out of my depth or unable to cope with anyone or anything, and I no longer fluctuate between wildly happy and excitable and deeply wounded, dragging myself off the floor in a tired effort simply to exist. I'm on an even keel, a position I never imagined I would achieve.

As you embark upon life sober, my advice would be to expect to feel deeply uncomfortable with your emotions for a few weeks, months or maybe even the primary year spent without drinking. The first time you feel anger, sadness or joy unfettered will be the most intense; after that and with time, those feelings will not result in the same depth of skin crawling strangeness. The emotions will seem less alien to you and you will grow to recognise them better, knowing how to deal with them successfully and soberly.

Don't be afraid to *feel* your emotions. A helpful phrase that I kept in mind initially (and still do in moments of sadness or stress) is 'This too shall pass', for all our feelings are fleeting – they enter in and out of our minds and bodies like the tide, ebbing and flowing, and ultimately disappearing. What we believe to be an overwhelming sense of anything will gradually wane and become manageable – a memory of a difficult time that we survived. And the old adage, 'What doesn't kill you will make you stronger' is worth remembering, too. As time passes, I have built up reserves of inner strength and coping mechanisms that often take me by surprise. There are rare instances when I forget I've grown so much emotionally, and I expect that fifteen-year-old response to leap out and stuff things up for me. Well, guess what? That girl became an adult, and the transition began just as soon as she put down the bottle.

It's nicely summarised in the title of this chapter – 'Feel, Deal, Heal'. Feel the emotion by being aware and mindful. Deal with it by not running away; instead, cry, scream, talk, cry some more and then do whatever works for you in helping yourself deal with it. It might be running, meditating or taking the dog for a walk – it may just be locking yourself in the bathroom and shutting out the world for a few minutes.

And finally, heal. Show yourself some compassion, understand what led you to feeling that particular emotion in the first place, recognise your human qualities and give yourself a break. And then move on. As time ticks on, this habit of working through feelings instead of stamping on them with a vat load of booze will change you from the inside out. And, one day, you'll recall the person you were as a drinker and hardly even know them as the one you've become.

G

Great Outdoors: Medicine for the Soul

When I was a child my family would regularly go for a drive as a leisure activity. This would usually occur at the weekend and more often than not when it was raining which, in 1980s Sheffield where I grew up, meant there was very little else to do other than play with my Sindy dolls or Spirograph. These drives would be exclusively countryside-based, the four of us cruising around the Peak District in our Volkswagen Jetta, idling away an hour or two prior to returning home where my sister and I would resume the Sindy doll/Spirograph fun.

I despised going for a drive; I found it to be pointless and utterly boring. The main reason for this was that I didn't entirely see the attraction of the great outdoors – particularly when it was tipping it down and I was trapped in the back of a car.

There were many other times as a child that I spent in a variety of green or mountainous environments which, although I didn't dislike them as much as the country drives, I had no true appreciation of at all. It wasn't until I'd spent a few years as an adult being ground down by a hectic, overcrowded city life that the penny dropped and I finally understood why my parents had felt so compelled to whisk us off in the Jetta and drive around the wilderness in the rain.

By the time I became a mother myself, I was well versed in the art of going for a drive, bundling my baby into her car seat and zooming off to admire the rural surroundings on the periphery of Sheffield. Despite the fact that it's not all that easy to embark on the type of long walks I favour while carrying a baby, I would find easily accessible locations that meant I was enjoying a blast of the countryside regardless. And yet still I didn't completely acknowledge what it is to be submerged in nature – that came much later, at a time when I had been sober for a few years.

There's something about the great outdoors that humbles me in a monumental way. When I first passed my driving test aged seventeen, I adored the freedom of being able to take myself off to isolated moorland areas where I would sit and cogitate over whatever issues were bothering me at the time (and there were always a substantial number). The vast expanse of land, unspoilt by the surge in population growth of the last couple of hundred years and the dominant capitalist agenda, was to me (and still is) calming, peaceful and pure.

Throughout my latter teenage years, the Peak District became my sanctuary. I'd sit and stare at the rocky crags and hills blanketed in heather and rhododendron bushes, contemplating this environment that had endured millennia. While I was stressing over a boyfriend dumping me or because I had put on a couple of pounds in weight, here was a huge area of solitude that had witnessed natural events of a magnitude so great I couldn't summon them to mind. It was as though time had abruptly stopped forging ahead, as if nothing had changed since dinosaurs roamed the Earth. The great outdoors has, for many years, provided me with this: an instant leap backwards to a less complicated age.

But when I became alcohol-free, I found myself connecting to the countryside in a way that I hadn't previously.

It stemmed originally from an understanding that, for decades, I had been unwittingly manipulated by the alcohol industry, and when this realisation hit, it was as though some heavy-duty blinkers were removed. Not only did I acknowledge that all the wine I'd dutifully bought and consumed was not, as I had allowed myself to believe, a means of meeting my aspirations (shallow, yes, I know, but I did quite fancy myself as a sophisticated connoisseur), I realised wine was merely a commodity, marketed and sold as a lifestyle choice, a supposed way of achieving intangible goals about the type of person I wanted to be. I saw that. And along with the alcohol blinkers I ditched blinkers to all sorts of other things.

As a society we are perpetually subjected to a tidal wave of ideals. The television is an endless source of advertising and promotion, telling us how we should be living and how we should look, what we should be eating and the type of car we should be driving.

Films are loaded with product placements, and billboards shout down at us as we walk beneath them, influencing us with perfect images depicting the type of life we are informed we should be leading.

And all of this bullshit, these many layers of nonsense, amounts to nothing of any great significance in the grand scheme of things. We are programmed to think it does – that the newest pair of trainers will transform us into cool and hip, or a particular model of car will magically make us appear sexy and powerful. It's cold manipulation that taps into the heart of our insecurities, and it is all for one common purpose: the pursuit of wealth. Once I had appreciated the alcohol industry as simply a vehicle for profits, I felt free to make my own choices, which brought me to feeling inner peace for the first time in my adult life.

Some of this I think has to do with age – advertisers are well aware that the young are the most easily influenced because they have a much more pronounced desire to conform and impress. This ebbs a little as we mature, and for me it did so with a rapid intensity just as soon as I put down the bottle.

And the environment where I now feel happiest, where I like to go to clear my head and where none of the above can encroach on either my conscious or unconscious mind, is the great outdoors. There are no corporate sponsored areas or franchised coffee outlets in the Peak District. The paths are the product of thousands upon thousands of feet trooping along between the boulders and clumps of heather and are the only true sign that humans have been anywhere near the place.

Over the years, my retreats to the great outdoors have become more of a necessity than a distraction. I crave a life as free and as honest to our ancient roots as possible, and although it's not an option for many to escape capitalist society completely, I find that if I balance the busyness of modern life with frequent immersions in the natural wilderness of the Peak District, then I can mitigate somewhat the negative effects the former has upon me.

On another more practical level, many of us rely on alcohol to ease our stresses. Although heavy drinking will inevitably create further stress and problems in our lives, it does unarguably present itself as a means of inducing a sense of shoulder-dropping relaxation. After a hectic day spent juggling all the tasks we are routinely faced with, a large glass of something alcoholic can be all too tempting as a way to ameliorate the tension. Therefore, when we stop drinking, it's vital that we find an immediate replacement for this coping strategy, and in my opinion, getting out into the countryside provides an effective solution.

And if there is no internet connection or phone signal, even better. In addition to the bombardment of the media, we are all now subjected to continual bothering by our mobile phones. Recently I've started leaving mine upstairs out of sight, otherwise I find myself drawn to the thing like a magnet, tapping away at the screen, checking social media or text messages, or browsing the internet for things I don't especially want, let alone need. And it creeps in; it's another way in which our minds are lost to the agenda of another person or a corporation aiming to manipulate our behaviour to suit their own gains – we need to possess things or change our appearance, own a bigger car or have whiter teeth. It creates more stress and worry. So ditching the whole toxic lot by temporarily relocating to the great outdoors, where you can be free to be your own person without being hassled by anyone or anything, where you can remind yourself of just how fast our time on the planet passes by, and where you can witness birds and animals that simply are without any worries or desires to be something they aren't, is medicine for the soul.

Studies into the Japanese concept of *shinrin-yoku*, or forest bathing, have shown that this practice of visiting forests for relaxation and recreational purposes has real benefits in terms of stress management. Originally proposed in 1982 by the Forest Agency of Japan, research into the efficacy of *shinrin-yoku* appears to support the notion that we can improve our general wellbeing if we incorporate regular visits to forests as part of a healthy lifestyle. Specifically, studies have proven that exposure to forests has a positive effect on the nervous system, resulting in an increased sense of calm. Upon visiting forests, a particular hormone (adiponectin) increases, low concentration of which is linked with type 2 diabetes and obesity. Studies into *shinrin-yoku* have also demonstrated links between the practice and a reduction in anger, stress, depression and sleeplessness.

For me, a feeling of wellbeing arises from the very fact that I have temporarily escaped the restraints and pressures of the modern world. Out in the Peak District there are no boundaries or expectations, just the wild – a place in which I can reconnect to our ancient heritage and where I am simply allowed to be. As a means of de-stressing, a brilliant solution for dealing with alcohol cravings in the early days, and a place where we are free to be human again, the great outdoors remains a very important element of my alcohol-free armoury.

H

Hobbies and Holidays

Urrghh, hobbies. What a boring word. What a boring thing to do. Hobbies are for dullards with nothing better to do with their time.

Wrong!

Very occasionally I am beset with terribly gloomy thoughts relating to the reality of life and death – that we are all going to die; that in millions of years there will be nothing left of any of us except perhaps some space dust. When these morbid ideas pop into my head, I find it unnervingly simple to reduce everything in the world to a state of pointlessness. I mean, when the Earth is no longer a planet and the stars have all burnt out, there will be no significance whatsoever attached to anything we've ever achieved or enjoyed in our lifetimes, will there?

Obviously we can't live our lives with the constant thought that we are, one day, going to pop our clogs because we'd never bother doing anything, caring for anything or anyone, or even getting out of bed in the morning. Albert Einstein once said, 'There are two ways to live: you can live as if nothing is a miracle; you can live as if everything is a miracle', and this is what I tell myself whenever the aforementioned gloominess sets in. As children we are predisposed to perceiving everything as wondrous, and then adulthood creeps in and it all, sadly, turns a little sour. Or at least, it does if we allow it to.

And for those of us who position alcohol on a pedestal, who prioritise drinking over most other activities, hobbies can seem more than a little bit meaningless – distractions to while away the hours as we await the onset of old age. Drinking copious amounts of alcohol, on the other hand, is a worthwhile exercise and a good use of our time. After all, we are socialising, relaxing and letting our hair down – or so we like to think.

The problem with boozing as a pastime, however, is that it can, for people who are unable to moderate their intake terribly well, lead to a number of seriously negative consequences that impact on multiple areas of their lives. It doesn't end with a night involving a few drinks; often it creates problems within our relationships, reduces our self-confidence and self-esteem, costs a lot of money from which we see little, if any, return, and acutely damages our health.

Regular drinking also occupies vast amounts of our time. From the planning to the imbibing to the recovery the following day, a heavy consumption of alcohol tends to dominate our lives. It leaves no spare hours whatsoever for pursuing any other activities – and besides, anything that doesn't involve booze is surely a complete waste of time and something to be avoided like the plague, isn't it?

Here, then, are the two most substantial reasons that I had no interest in hobbies for my entire adult life until I stopped drinking: firstly, if it didn't involve booze then I didn't want to be doing it, and secondly, hobbies are a stupid waste of time and something that only dull people do.

But then I became a non-drinker, and none of the above applied any longer. Hobbies, I quickly realised, are not just distractions but an excellent means of achieving numerous other goals. For a start, many pastimes (booze-free, of course) will necessarily involve interacting with other people. If you sign up to a writing class or join a gym, partake in a regular film or book club or learn how to rock climb, you will be meeting new faces, some of whom may well become friends. These people will probably not hold alcohol in quite as high regard as you have always done, hence their interest in your chosen activity (or maybe they will be exactly like you, looking for alcohol-free ways to spend their time because they too want to be sober on a permanent basis). All of this will aid your booze-free endeavours enormously, as well as providing a welcome distraction from drinking in the early days when the cravings are still hitting in frequent tidal waves.

In addition to making interesting new friends who don't consider booze to be the be-all and end-all (which in itself will help boost your confidence), taking part in a hobby will help increase your self-belief. This is because you will be trying something different and gradually proving to yourself you're capable of things that you previously thought you couldn't manage. There is an immense rush of satisfaction to be found in reaching targets – being able to converse comfortably in a foreign language or running for several miles after being unfit for years, for example, are achievements that will spur you on and help create a feeling of inner strength and invincibility. They will reignite the exciting sense of potential (most likely buried after years of drinking excessively) that we all possess in our youth – the dreams we once regarded as entirely within our grasp, but which, as we mature into adults, somehow wither away to nothing.

Partaking in a hobby works wonders for the soul. Just because the thought of crocheting or collecting stamps might send you into a deep slumber, you shouldn't assume that all pastimes will be of no interest to you. There is something for everyone; it's just a matter of discovering what that may be for you.

I am passionate about writing and exercising, spending time with my children and our dog. I love animals and bird watching, and I derive great pleasure from being out in the countryside. I also, once I became alcohol-free, began baking again – something I adored as a child but which, once the booze bus came along, got side-lined along with so many other activities I had once enjoyed. And while, admittedly, I did engage in most of these interests when I was a drinker, it was with limited enthusiasm and vigour, largely because they simply got in the way of my passion for wine. Even the cinema was an inconvenience as it equated to a night out without alcohol – or, at the very best, only a couple of drinks squeezed in either side of the film which was, quite frankly, deeply frustrating.

The pastimes I enjoy now as a non-drinker are ones to which I apply myself fully. If I'm out walking in the hills, it is this and only this that demands my attention. I'm not thinking of pints of beer in a country pub, or contemplating how much drinking time I'll have left when I arrive home as a result of wasting hours marching about unnecessarily in the countryside. When I'm baking with my younger daughter, it isn't with one eye on the clock, wishing the hours away in order to reach her bedtime and my wine o'clock. And if I am writing, I am doing so with pure concentration as opposed to harbouring feelings of resentment, because really all I want to do is switch off my laptop and get stuck into a bottle.

If there's one thing all heavy drinkers have in common it is that they occupy a miniscule world. Alcohol consumption (when it's regular and intense) shrinks our existence, creating a daily schedule based on nothing more than getting pissed and subsequently recovering. Meeting new friends is, quite honestly, exhausting – unless they too are only interested in getting sloshed, and then it's irrelevant whom we are talking to because all parties present are inebriated. Anything that doesn't involve drinking is abandoned for obvious reasons, and activities that demand concentration and commitment are a total waste of time, as who can deliver such attributes when half cut?

But hobbies, when one is alcohol-free, broaden horizons – they help to expand an individual's world. Doing nothing is tolerable when you are drinking to cushion the tedium of it; take the alcohol away and being bored is quite awful. This tends to force the non-drinker out of his or her comfort zone and into new activities, enjoyed alongside different people and in previously uncharted territory. There is nowhere to hide when you are stone cold sober – it becomes essential to fill empty evenings and weekends with something constructive. And although it might feel as scary as hell, doing it should provoke the desire to keep doing it, to push on further in order to find out exactly what you are capable of.

And so to holidays, which are, to the average heavy boozer, a perfect excuse for an extended piss-up. Most people who are alcohol-dependent will only usually stall a drinking session due to various unavoidable obstacles and restrictions: work, children and the desire not to be perceived as a hopeless drunk. Remove these standard daily interruptions to one's alcohol consumption, and what are you left with? That's correct: a holiday.

People are allowed to drink a lot on holiday – that is to say, boozy behaviour from those jetting off to sunnier climes is considered socially acceptable. How many of us have witnessed fellow travellers downing pints of lager in the airport at some ungodly hour before the sun has even risen? When I drank alcohol, I would routinely consume two or three large glasses of wine during my time spent at the airport and on board the plane. This was, I reassured myself, purely down to my fear of flying and was, therefore, entirely justified.

And once we arrive at our chosen destination, we frequently feel entitled to enjoy a few drinks to help us unwind and really make the holiday go with a bang. We are not required to be up early in the mornings, everyone is generally more relaxed, and thus alcohol seems to suit the mood perfectly.

The issue here (once again) for those of us devoid of the off-switch is that we do not drink like other people do. Beginning with a higher level of 'acceptable' than your average moderate drinker, our holiday drinking can quickly escalate to monumental proportions. If a bottle of wine a night is standard when at home, the vacation equivalent is likely to exceed three bottles. And this is not an ingredient for a happy holiday for anyone present.

What, then, is the newly teetotal person to expect when travelling for the first time minus a steady flow of booze to fill up all the unwanted cracks in their happiness? Because let's face it, if you have always consumed alcohol as an adult then all your holidays will have been booze-fuelled weeks of mayhem. And if you're anything like me as a drinker, alcohol was the whole point of a holiday.

I believe there are some hard and fast rules to help the people for whom this book was written (i.e. those who are incapable of moderating their consumption and are learning how to live without booze) enjoy alcohol-free holidays. You probably will not be able to incorporate all of the following into your next holiday, or even the one after that. Like much of life after drinking, adjustments will take time, effort and planning. But if you work towards these aims, you'll get there eventually and so will be able to look forward to feeling content and rejuvenated during and after your future holidays – which is far preferable to arriving home with the mother of all hangovers and nothing to show for your fortnight away except an extra spare tyre and bags the size of suitcases under your eyes.

AF Holiday Rule #1: Choose a location that interests you. Frankly, when you drink a lot, you could be holidaying on a landfill site and you wouldn't notice all that much (at least, not after you'd sunk the first couple of jugs of Sangria). However, things are wildly different when you are completely sober; in fact, the exact opposite is true. You'll really notice your environment, and it will become, apart from the break from working and the company of whomever you are holidaying with, the most important element of your time away.

Since I quit alcohol, I've picked locations that are historically, culturally or geographically interesting to me. I also look for places conducive to fitness activities such as cycling, hiking, surfing or skiing as I love all of these things and engaging daily in any of them is my idea of heaven. My worst nightmare would be a noisy, bar-filled resort, rammed with people all seeking a mental escape. But whatever rocks your boat! Just make sure that wherever you go, you're going to enjoy it for what it has to offer other than booze.

AF Holiday Rule #2: Go on holiday with people you like. This may prove difficult for some as alcohol conceals all sorts of dissatisfactions – not least an unhappy relationship. When we are drinking heavily, it detracts from the true dynamic of a partnership; take the booze away and giant holes could be revealed, especially on holiday where the everyday busyness of life comes to a standstill. Aside from our partner, there are also friends to consider. As discussed earlier in the book, we usually choose similarly heavy drinkers in our social circles when we ourselves drink – precisely the type of people we wouldn't want to spend a week with sober.

If you are planning on being a non-drinker on a permanent basis, it may be necessary to cut loose some friends and even your partner, should the incompatibilities become unmanageable without the veil of alcohol disguising them. Holidays should be fun and relaxing, and they will be if you are with the right person or people. A week away in close quarters with someone you can barely stand to be in the same room with will amount to a hellish experience.

AF Holiday Rule #3: Avoid places with memories of drinking copious amounts. As a teenager I visited Faliraki and Kavos, both in Greece and both with the infamous 18-30 Holiday company. Booze cruises, bar crawling, scooting about on the back of boys' mopeds while wearing a tiny bikini and being fairly hammered – I partook in all of the average English person's Mediterranean holiday clichés. As the years progressed I visited many cities, mountains, beaches and picturesque villages, and in most of them I carved out some reasonably distressing alcohol-related memories.

I would advise avoiding like the plague any holiday location that will remind you of drinking until you have at least a couple of AF years under your belt. Triggers will be firing off at an alarming rate if you descend on a place where, in days gone by, you would have been getting quietly sloshed in a little bar somewhere, or necking piña coladas on the beach beneath a particularly pleasing palm tree. The sun, the omission of restrictions (work being the main one), together with the strong impulse to let your hair down because you are on holiday could all prove too much to withstand. Go easy on yourself and pick a new destination with no drinking memories – good or bad.

AF Holiday Rule #4: Find time to meditate. You'll have more free hours on holiday than you do at home so there's no excuse for not doing this. Devote a few minutes every morning to meditating, repeating a mantra pertaining to using your holiday to relax and recharge your batteries, and you'll really help yourself stay focused on this goal. Meditation aids mindfulness and encourages a sense of calm – remind yourself each day that relaxation is the reason why you are on holiday and you'll be prioritising it clearly in your mind, which, in turn, will assist you throughout the day to achieve this aim.

AF Holiday Rule #5: Be a bit selfish. You work your bum off all year, traipsing round after other people, picking things up and washing their clothes, restocking the fridge and cleaning the loo. Then you go on holiday and, if you aren't careful, you end up doing exactly the same thing there. This endless domestic slog results (unsurprisingly) in major feelings of resentment and bitterness. And both of these emotions are especially helpful in pushing you towards the wine section of the local supermarket.

My advice would be to pre-empt this and outline expectations pre-holiday with your nearest and dearest. Explain that this is your holiday too and you deserve and need a rest, just like your travel companions. Work out how best to achieve a holiday from which everyone benefits and, if necessary, pencil in a few hours here and there just for you where you do the things you love doing, free from the responsibilities of the kids or whoever else you're going away with.

Hobbies and holidays are equally brilliant for injecting passion and excitement back into your life once the alcohol has been shelved. Work at embracing them. If you run from them, too frightened to try your hand at anything new, you'll be missing out on vast amounts of enjoyment and satisfaction. Both hobbies and holidays will boost your personal growth, helping to build confidence and self-esteem, and could lead you to new adventures that you never imagined in your wildest dreams. The key to having a good time without booze is to live in the moment, and we will look at this in more detail in the chapter on mindfulness later in the book.

I

Identify With Someone Who Does Sober Well

Everything in life works best when in a balanced state, when extremes are avoided and we can apply a degree of moderation. I seem to have a proclivity for excess, but since quitting the booze I have been working very hard at managing it and striving for a steadier approach to things. (Incidentally, I have long since paid no attention whatsoever to astrology, largely because my star sign is Libra, illustrated by a pair of scales and thus being so wildly unlike my character that I cannot possibly believe it to hold any basis in reality.)

This is why I amended the title of this chapter from 'Idolise Someone Who Does Sober Well' to 'Identify With Someone Who Does Sober Well'. Idolise implies infatuation, placing too great an emphasis on the actions of another person, whereas what this section is really about is finding a fellow teetotaller who makes sense to you, who has the potential to inspire you. In other words, look to someone you like and admire to observe (in a healthy manner) how they do sobriety.

When I came to the life-changing conclusion that I could no longer continue to drink alcohol (at least, not if I wanted to live and be happy), my biggest fear lay in my (erroneous) belief that I would be transformed, via the lack of booze, into a purposeless, personality-free zone with no friends and no social life. I failed to envisage the type of person I would be as a non-drinker, 'I' being the operative word in this sentence. Forget notions of boring farts who don't drink because they are frightened of living; forget the religious people who don't touch a drop because God forbids it; forget the zealous health nuts whose lives revolve around a strict code of regimented dos and don'ts with regard to what is allowed to pass their lips. This was about *me*, and how sobriety would work for me, just as it is now about *you* and the sort of person you will be without alcohol. Who you were as a drinker and who you will become without alcohol are not entirely separate entities. There are crossovers, fragments of your character that will remain without the booze, bits that will improve and flourish. And then there are the parts that will dissipate and fade away – the bits of you that only existed as a consequence of the falsity of heavy drinking. It's crucial not to be afraid of yourself as a human being living free from mind-altering substances.

When I was growing up I had numerous idols, mainly musicians. Their faces were plastered all over my bedroom walls on huge floor-to-ceiling posters: Shaun Ryder, Robert Smith, Ian Brown and Anthony

Kiedis (Red Hot Chili Peppers). How they lived and what they stood for provided a blueprint for my own behaviour because I admired them; I wanted to be just like them. Without a scrap of regret, I can link fairly conclusively my adoration of some of these people (and others of a similar ilk) with my teenage dalliances in drug-taking and heavy boozing. Living the rock 'n' roll lifestyle was something that resonated with me; it felt correct for me to be that person – the rebel and the wild girl who got such a thrill out of living dangerously.

As I've matured, I've noticed that this tendency to seek out idols has not disappeared entirely, although I no longer have posters stuck all over my bedroom walls. I want to know that people I admire and respect are still out there because it reassures me that the world is a good place and I'm not swimming alone in a sea of unfamiliarity. Frequently, I pause and observe our cultural landscape only to see endless examples of things that hold no significance to me at all – people who are shallow, obsessed with celebrity status and not much else. And so the shining lights of optimism out there, singing from the same hymn sheet as me, are of huge importance, whether they stem from the arena of politics or music. It is a comfort to witness those who speak the same language as me – as it is for any of us. We all need to feel represented by someone.

When it comes to lifestyle choices, quitting booze is right up there with the biggies. Almost everyone in western society drinks alcohol – albeit maybe not to excess on a regular basis. For most people, downing a few drinks is an essential prerequisite for a night out (or a special evening in). It can feel fairly isolating to announce that, all of a sudden, you will no longer be partaking. And this is a major factor in why people sometimes return to their old boozy ways after just a few weeks on the wagon – it feels wrong to be the odd one out. It can be uncomfortable and feel as though we've drifted away from that which has always been so easy and familiar.

This is where the person whom you admire for how he or she lives the sober life comes in very handy. There's a common expression bandied about among those who are now alcohol-free but who used to drink too much: 'Fake it until you make it'. I can highly recommend abiding by this motto, and if you need some guidance in what exactly you're supposed to be faking then look no further than your sober role model (whoever that may be) for some ideas.

When I first stopped drinking, I had no idea how to be. The tiniest of details in just being were of huge importance to me. I remember going out one night with a big group (some of whom I knew very well and others who were virtually strangers to me) for a meal. One of the women in the group, a friend's sister, was a non-drinker. She was stylish and pretty with a quirky dress sense that matched her personality – a little off the wall, but in a nice, non-threatening way. I watched her in certain situations which, to me back then, made me feel completely awkward: ordering a drink (that wasn't alcoholic), talking to people (without being drunk and loud) and announcing that she was leaving for home (driving herself as opposed to being poured into a black cab by concerned but somewhat weary friends). It was like reading a manual, and all the time I was thinking to myself, oh! So that's how you do it. It can be done – you can be nice and interesting when you are stone cold sober.

I contacted somebody else who I knew had had real problems with booze prior to quitting several years before I did. Funnily enough, I used to drink with her quite a bit in my early to mid-twenties, and I often remarked back then on her apparent inability to call it a day, even when I myself was getting rip-roaring drunk far too frequently – a fine example of denial in action! But anyway, I met up with this woman who had used AA and the Twelve Steps model to carve out her own alcohol-free life, and she became another person whom I looked to (informally) for guidance in how to be sober. We met for a coffee and she filled me in on her newfound love of yoga, and how much calmer and happier she was now that she no longer consumed alcohol. I was amazed at the difference in her, and thought very clearly, I want to feel like this, too. She taught me that not drinking could be a good thing a long time before I felt that way myself.

Deep within me, there was an embryonic belief that living without alcohol had to be an improvement on drinking every day, but I couldn't fully accept it for quite some time after I quit. On many occasions I was screaming at myself internally to trust it, stay with it and keep focused on what I might become if I just stayed sober, and the people I observed in those early days helped me immeasurably. They provided me with a model for how to exist and still be a person I could like once the alcohol had been taken away.

In addition to the women I knew personally, I also turned once again to musicians for inspiration on how I wanted to live, only this time I was looking to the ones who used to get wasted but had now sobered up. Of all the people in the world I most admire, it is musicians who relentlessly inspire me, effortlessly demanding adoration and worship from me in the same way a god can from a believer. Their creativity, combined with living a life of total freedom as opposed to towing the line and conforming to societal expectations, is what I find the most compelling about my musical heroes.

And so, early on in my newly sober world, I found myself persistently drawn to the recordings of Johnny Cash, someone whose music I'd always loved, but whose personal history then became deeply poignant and significant to my own journey. Reflected in Cash's songs are sorrow, humility and his widely documented struggles for redemption and release from the cast-iron bars of self-hatred that drove him to alcohol and drug taking, and they spoke out to me with unequivocal resonance. Johnny Cash's expansive career culminated in his recording of a cover of the Nine Inch Nails track 'Hurt' which, although not penned by Cash, is powerfully evocative of his own experiences.

Much of my feeling of connection with Cash was born out of my desperation to make sense of my alcohol dependency and work out who I was without booze blurring my reality. I felt for a long time that I'd never be able to forgive myself for the way I had acted on several occasions when drunk. Those horrific, soul-destroying memories that stick like glue and threaten to erode any chance of developing a fraction of self-esteem appeared, for a while, to be permanent fixtures within my consciousness. But Johnny Cash, with his heart-wrenching introspection and, for much of his life, severe self-hatred, sang lyrics that seemed to sew up the holes in my heart.

I found myself reasoning that here was a man whom I admired greatly, despite the fact that for so long he didn't care much for himself, drank too much and used drugs. And therefore, if I could view him in such a positive light, perhaps I should also recognise some good in me.

I know there was a world of difference between my consumption of white wine (mainly) and the heroin habit that took hold of Anthony Kiedis's life for years. My settee, for the most part being the rather banal setting for my Pinot Grigio/Chablis consumption, was a far cry from downtown Los Angeles, the city in which Kiedis struggled with (and consequently highlighted in numerous songs) his heroin addiction. It's hardly the same thing – is it? And yet, in the words of 'Other Side' and 'Scar Tissue' I saw myself and my own battles with substance misuse and the associated misery it inflicted on my life. Kiedis's rise from the ashes and ultimate conquering of his habit provided me with proof that someone can move on from their drug and/or alcohol misuse to become a sober yet still eminently cool (in my opinion) person. I still listen to the Red Hot Chili Peppers and they remain my favourite band. Their take on the world resonates with me; their music makes total sense to me.

Over the course of the last five years, during which time I've not touched a drop of alcohol, I've become a content and balanced individual. I now have a healthy level of self-confidence – I actually like the person I've grown into, a novelty after an entire adult lifetime of not liking myself much at all. And a significant stepping-stone that got me here was seeking inspiration and guidance from the sober people I came across, both in real life and ones I admired from afar. Remember, fake it until you make it, and if you need to know what to fake, there's no better learning resource than a person you find appealing who is an accomplished non-drinker.

J

Just Be Yourself

In all of the hundreds of blogs on Soberistas that I've read over the last few years, I've noticed a theme among us problem drinkers. A large number of those writing seem to be in a permanent state of discomfort and unease around people they are not overly familiar with. Furthermore, many of us harbour a sense of not being good enough, of feeling inferior to our peers, perhaps even a fraud. This pops up especially frequently in posts written on the subject of employment, where adults in their thirties, forties and fifties admit to doubting their status in the workplace, despite having achieved a reasonable to high level of success and being ostensibly well-liked by colleagues.

Where does this uncertainty stem from? Are we born this way, hence the common attraction to alcohol as a means of ameliorating this uncomfortable state of being? Is it the excessive alcohol consumption that contributes to the inferiority complex, or a combination of the two?

For me, the notion of not quite making the grade began inching its way into my conscious mind around the age of twelve. I would always describe myself as possessing a stubborn and fairly dominant streak, but since my early teens this has been tempered by the persistent and nagging suspicion that I was not as good as other people. At its worst, this feeling reached epic proportions, rendering me incapable of facing the most innocuous of interactions like paying a bus driver my fare, or even leaving the house. It has filled me with self-doubt and panic in social situations when I've compared my physical self with other women I perceived to be far more attractive than I was.

With regard to my academic achievements, I have repeatedly played down any that were above average. When I obtained a high grade for the postgraduate law degree I completed in 2010, I told myself it was because the paper was too easy. Anyone could have done the same. When it came to jobs, I always aimed low, playing it safe and never pushing myself further than I thought I deserved to.

Much of this lack of confidence arose out of a core feeling of not being the same as other people. I felt out of place much of the time, a spare part – as if the rest of society had been granted access to a private set of rules and conventions of behaviour that had somehow passed me by. I felt slightly weird, an oddball. I was on the periphery, permanently looking for acceptance from the popular group. Underpinning this entire phenomenon was the notion that the real me was not acceptable and I must alter myself if I was ever to fit in with the mainstream of humanity.

Alongside this severe lack of self-esteem, I drifted into numerous relationships in my younger years with people who were not at all compatible with me. I had no real idea about who I was, what made me tick, the qualities I desperately needed in friends and partners, the activities that would have filled me with contentment and satisfaction. Perhaps, most importantly, I didn't have a grasp on the fact that I had a major proclivity towards addictive and extreme behaviours. I never considered myself to be someone with problems when it came to drugs and booze. Rather, I subconsciously nurtured an alter ego that allowed me to indulge in mind-altering substances and pursue romantic dalliances with people who were totally ill-suited to me. And this extraneous version of myself was the one that gradually came to represent who I was, in my entirety.

It was, therefore, with a monumental jolt that I returned to a sense of reality upon quitting alcohol in 2011. Over the months that followed my last drink, I came to appreciate that actually the 'me' who I thought was real was nothing more than a drug- and alcohol-fuelled hallucination. She simply didn't exist beyond the parameters of the pub or the wine aisle of the supermarket. In the non-artificial existence of the sober person, I suddenly found myself (or at least the old version of me) to be obsolete.

So what was left behind?

Well, much of the stuff that was there from my childhood remained. I learnt that I am strong-willed (not necessarily the terrible characteristic that I had often considered it to be once I'd morphed into adulthood); creative (God only knows where that particular quality disappeared to, but it sure as hell vanished like a puff of smoke the minute I began drinking); thoughtful (I always regarded myself as a selfish and thoughtless person as a drinker); interested in learning and growing (dumbing down and keeping it simple had generally been the order of the day during my boozy life). Perhaps the most significant change to my personality has been the fact that over time (and this has been a very gradual process) my self-confidence has re-emerged. I became aware of this as the gap closed between me and other people – the ones whom I had always compared myself with so unfavourably. Without alcohol, I could sense a burgeoning equality, which today is absolute. I no longer feel overwhelmed with a desire for the floor to swallow me up whenever I'm in new company. I can hold my own, safe in the knowledge that I am just as worthy a human being as the next person. I can look people in the eye when I am speaking with them.

In the old drinking days I would plough effort into altering myself, trying to blend in with everyone else by emphasising the elements of my personality I considered more acceptable, while siphoning off the bits that I felt were out of the realm of social norms. I didn't have the confidence to be me, free from the prop of alcohol.

Allowing yourself to be you has something to do with the ageing process as well. We are less inclined to feel the pressure of expectation as we mature – hence the great expense of corporations in predominantly targeting the youth market through advertising. With an increased sense of mortality, we attach far less importance to following the latest fashion trends and a greater significance on focusing on our loved ones or pursuing decades-old dreams. What other people think of us matters less and we are generally happier to allow nature to take its course.

But excessive alcohol consumption feeds into the notion that we are less equal to others because it erodes our self-esteem and exacerbates a feeling of nervy paranoia. You may have experienced jangling nerves the morning after a heavy drinking session, jumping at the slightest noise and feeling as though your emotions have been scrubbed raw. Alcohol disrupts the natural order of our emotional wellbeing, and coupled with the fact we regularly act when drunk in ways that leave us embarrassed or deeply ashamed the following morning, the physiological depressive effects of binge-drinking create a wrecking ball-sized impact on our levels of self-worth.

It is a natural state of affairs that in our early teenage years we feel somewhat out of sorts, self-conscious because of puberty and filled with longing to be like everyone else. It's a bizarre chapter in our lives when the apron strings are cut and our parents cease to be the be-all and end-all of our worlds. Alcohol is thrust in our faces at exactly the moment when its abilities to boost confidence (albeit falsely and temporarily) and make us feel invincible are most desirable. And for the people with a predisposition for alcohol dependency (due to genetic and/or social factors), drinking is steadily and seamlessly incorporated into everyday life.

Drinking on a regular basis inevitably alters our personalities. It turns us into people we wouldn't have become had we never consumed alcohol. It blocks developments in our thinking that would otherwise have taken place and it prevents us from fully experiencing our emotions. Therefore, when we choose at a later date to stop drinking, there will, undoubtedly, be a fallout. Knowing who you really are won't occur overnight. Learning to distinguish between the elements of yourself that were purely born out of alcohol misuse and those that are an inherent part of you and will remain post-drinking will take time, too. The period immediately after you begin your alcohol-free life will likely leave you feeling in a state of flux – personally I felt as though I had no personality whatsoever, as if I'd been wiped clean like marker pen being rubbed off a whiteboard.

The trick to working all of this out, however, is patience. Do not worry too much about what's around the corner. Had I known then what I know now, I would have viewed that time in my own life with complete excitement and optimism. It was a fresh start – a moment when I was finally able to let go of all the falsity and wrong choices that drinking had brought into my existence and embrace living in a manner that was true to the person I really am. But, unaware of how much things were about to improve for me as a result of becoming a non-drinker, I was scared and unsure, and mostly kept myself to myself for as much time as I could get away with.

When we frequently drink a lot, we inevitably halt our personal development. Alcohol serves as a barrier to our emotional maturity, and not only that, because excessive consumption suppresses our self-esteem, we can find ourselves severely hampered in terms of the goals and expectations we have for our daily lives. The temptation to aim low is strong, as is withdrawal from any level of human interaction that ventures beyond basic and essential. Because we are alcohol dependent, we cocoon ourselves in a booze-friendly environment and usually stay within it, for the fear of stepping outside into a place that could restrict our drinking is very real.

Take the booze away, however, and an exciting transformation begins to occur. When we're no longer acting like drunken idiots, letting ourselves down in front of friends and family and then being forced to deal with the soul-destroying internal mayhem the next morning, we can start to repair some of the emotional bruising that has been going on for years. Gradually, we are able to perceive ourselves differently; we're not rotten to the core as we thought was the case when we were drinking all the time, saying hurtful things to the ones we love, letting them down on a regular basis and consequently reinforcing the notion that we are worthless. We are now putting other people first a little more, which sets the wheel of a virtuous circle in motion. Now our self-respect is re-emerging from a dark hole like an injured animal, battered and broken but crawling steadfastly towards safety. There are instances when we act positively in a particular way or say certain words, and it dawns on us that we would never have done or said such a thing back in our drinking days.

This strengthening of our inner character and self-confidence has an important secondary outcome: it helps us to recognise that what other people think of us doesn't matter so much – at least, not when it comes to the people we don't know and/or value in life. Again I think of that an old saying: 'Those who matter don't mind, and those who mind don't matter'. Taking this on board is suddenly a possibility when you are armed with self-esteem and confidence. You don't care all that much what complete strangers think of your choice of trousers, or how you speak, or the fact that you used to have an issue with booze and now you don't touch the stuff. It's easy to disregard the opinion of people who make glib judgements about us when we have the self-belief to know that we, too, are worthy human beings.

And this slow but unrelenting growth in our self-worth is like a wall being built. As it becomes higher, the potential for it to be brought down by an external attack is vastly reduced. Self-esteem prevents the erosion of our sense of self by other people's actions and comments. We become tougher and able to deal more effectively with challenging situations.

All of this results in a powerful conclusion: once self-esteem and confidence are restored, we are free just to be. The important word in that sentence is 'free' because freedom is what this whole process is about. Instead of being tied up in shackles, twisting and contorting ourselves in an effort to be what everyone around us wants us to be; instead of forbidding some elements of our persona to emerge because we are fearful of being judged harshly and disliked, we are free to show the world exactly who we are. The ones who don't like what they see were never true friends in the first place. These people we are able to let drift from our lives as we are no longer the clingy, frightened individual with no self-esteem we once were.

Be yourself – a concept that is a million miles away from the damaged and scared drinker yet a normal, simple and healthy state of being for those recovered from alcohol dependency. Many people on Soberistas share their disbelief with regard to their old self – the one who existed when they drank too much too often. When they gaze back in time and remember the fractured, terrified person they once were, they struggle to equate him or her with the person they've grown into. There's a disconnection, because the changes that have taken place have been so slow to come into effect they were barely noticeable, but then – wham! One day, it's all there – everything comes together and it was all worth the fight.

This is leap of faith time. You're not there yet, but you will be. You can't imagine it because you've never known it. You don't see who you will become because you've never met that person before. But he or she is there, right now, inside you, waiting to be released. And the only means of helping that inner you out is to stay alcohol-free. Trust me, you'll be so glad you did.

K

Kick Ass in the Gym
(Or Just Go For a Walk)

You may not want to read this chapter, especially if physical exercise has consistently been notable by its absence in your mental list of enjoyable activities. But what the hell, it's going in the book anyway because I am a firm believer in three things related to fitness:

- the mind and body are inextricably linked;

- physical activity is *the* best way to deal with stress and obtain a natural high;

- being fit and in shape massively boosts self-confidence.

It probably doesn't take a genius to pinpoint the connections between these three statements and drinking rather too much alcohol. Yes, when you feel crap physically, you will almost certainly experience a downturn in mood. When you are gagging for a drink because your stress levels are on red alert and you are so wound up there are veins popping out of your temples, getting stuck into some exercise will help enormously to deal with this urge. For those who have relied on alcohol and/or other substances in order to experience a mental high, it's a good idea to find a replacement source for this when you put down the bottle. And finally, when you feel rubbish about yourself, you are more likely to seek out mental obliteration via booze. As doing regular exercise bolsters confidence, those people who engage in it are far less likely to experience the urge to get hammered in the first place.

Before I continue, for those readers with an intense dislike for health nut types, I would like to present my credentials as a one-time exercise-hating, pizza-loving slob. Approximately three decades ago, I entered into secondary school, and it was there that I fostered a deep and fearful dislike of physical exercise. I did not enjoy throwing myself about upon the very large trampoline in front of all my classmates, male and female, owing to my newly-conspicuous breasts bouncing painfully whenever my feet left the unforgiving equipment. I did not especially care for the freezing cold showers and carbolic soap with which we were expected to scrub our pubescent bodies within full view of our (female only this time, thankfully) school friends post-exercise. And I did not feel any affection for the enforced rugby and football matches we played alongside the often-aggressive boys in my class. Quickly, I turned from a person who had a fairly ambivalent attitude towards exercise into one who utterly hated it. From that time onwards, I did everything in my power to duck out of PE class, and would even hide in a bush near the start of the school's cross-country runs with a couple of mates and a packet of fags. Here we would puff away and wait for the class to return after its three-mile jaunt, when we would tag on at the back as if we'd taken part in the entire event (reeking of cigarettes and believing ourselves to be very clever).

A few years later, I became a mother. This event had a profound effect upon me, in that I suddenly started to care about staying alive long enough to be there for my daughter as she grew up. Although this awakening did not, sadly, extend to my drinking habits back then, I did attempt to mitigate the alcohol by signing up to the Sheffield half marathon in 2001, launching myself accordingly into a training regime alongside my sister and a friend. Running appealed hugely to the twenty-five-year-old me, and I've continued to do it on a regular basis ever since. This chapter is about why.

Exercise should never be perceived as a punishing gym schedule that fills you with dread, or one that adds yet another chore to an already fit-to-burst daily routine and causes you to feel even more stressed. In order for fitness to become easy, it needs to be viewed positively – an enjoyable activity that you really look forward to. And this will not be the case if you fail to appreciate the three statements outlined at the beginning of this chapter.

Up until fairly recently in the history of our species, human beings were much more active than many are today. Obesity rates have exploded in the last few decades, with unhealthy diets and sedentary lifestyles being the major causes. As technical innovations continue to spring forth – both at home and in the workplace – the requirement for physically demanding work has dropped significantly. In addition, according to the World Health Organisation, thirty per cent of the global population does not get sufficient exercise. Both cars and televisions have contributed to this statistic, with people doing less activity and far more settee dwelling since the invention of both. Not only does all this lead to premature death due to heart disease, liver disease and type 2 diabetes (among other illnesses and diseases associated with being overweight), but obesity doesn't tend to do a great deal for a person's self-confidence either.

Put simply, we were not designed to sit still all day in front of a computer screen or television, eating heavily processed foods with a high salt and/or sugar content. If you have ever owned a dog and failed to walk it for a day or two, you will have probably noticed it going slightly round the twist and bombing about your house like a creature possessed. Take the dog for a walk and all is right with the world once more. This is how I perceive human beings – we are, after all, animals, and our bodies and minds work in unison to ensure we operate in the most effective way possible. So while we might not feel especially enthusiastic about putting on our trainers and getting outside for a brisk walk or run, we will definitely feel the benefits afterwards if we go ahead and do it, largely because of the production of the naturally produced chemicals, endorphins.

When I was a young mum and first began to run regularly, I quickly acknowledged its appeal as both a stress-buster and a route to feeling very joyful indeed. On more than the odd occasion, my sister, friend and I would conclude our run in fits of uncontrollable giggles as our individual endorphin rushes magnified a silly joke into something utterly hilarious. Two of us had toddlers at the time, and to escape the domestic grind for an hour while laughing our heads off and getting fit was a highly tempting option when faced with the alternative (feeding and bathing a tired, grouchy two-year-old at the end of a long day).

Here, then, we have some good general reasons for introducing exercise into your life: escaping the house and the associated domestic grind for a while, laughing more and maintaining a healthy weight. However, there are also several benefits to being more physically active specifically helpful to people aiming to kick the booze.

First of all, exercise is incredibly effective at banishing cravings. A craving will only last for approximately ten minutes, although in the midst of it, it can feel as though it's going on for an eternity. When you are subjected to the convincing voice of the Wine Witch/Addict Head/Monkey On Your Shoulder telling you, 'One drink won't hurt', it is incredibly difficult to believe it is not worth listening to. It sounds like you. It actually begins to make sense. It can be very hard to ignore.

Now, here is where exercise comes in. It's a distraction which simultaneously boosts your mood. And it helps to fill you up with all the stuff you really want in your life – energy, health and vitality – while letting go of all the bad things such as hangovers, regrets and self-loathing.

When I first quit drinking, I utilised running as my favourite tool against cravings. As soon as one hit (and they were regular and challenging for the first few months), I would get out into the woods near my house and run for half an hour. It didn't matter about achieving my personal best; it just mattered that I was away from home, outdoors in the fresh air and feeling instantly more positive in my fight against booze. By the time I returned home, the craving had gone and I was able to focus on other things.

As time goes on and exercise becomes a more frequent feature of your life, you should begin to notice the positive effects it is having on your body. Not only have the booze calories been laid to rest, the extra physical activity will almost certainly be helping tone you up. The impact this will have on your state of mind is massive. Rather than staring in the mirror at an overweight, bleary-eyed, depressed person (which, let's face it, is only going to make you want to drink even more), now you get to see a fitter, glowing, sexier version of you smiling back – an image that should really help motivate you in staying on the alcohol-free road.

Occasionally, I still ponder the inherent differences between people who cannot control their alcohol intake and the ones who have always been able to moderate with reasonable success. Whenever I now meet one of the latter, I can appreciate that the way he or she handles life just comes naturally. They were born that way, whereas for people who have struggled to beat an alcohol dependency, these strategies have to be learnt. For example, if someone who doesn't rely on booze to deal with stress or uncomfortable emotions seeks out a means to improve their mind-set, it will involve maybe phoning a friend for a chat, hitting the gym, or having a cup of tea and a read of a magazine. Not so for those who drink compulsively or regularly to excess. These people will automatically reach for a glass of something. So when you quit drinking, you need to arm yourself with the tools that people without alcohol problems employ. And exercise is probably the best one to turn to.

Another bonus of including physical exercise within your alcohol-free armoury is that it has the potential to provide you with some sober socialising. When you stop drinking, you are asking for trouble if your social life continues to revolve around the local pub with all the people you have always got pissed with, and for whom drinking huge amounts seems to pose no problems at all. You'll more than likely compare and contrast their still-drinking lives with your own dull one (as you will persuade yourself this is the case) and opt into the whole booze malarkey once again, but with added gusto. Or you'll feel utterly miserable and bereft about not being able to join them, and this too is bound to push you towards alcohol again before long.

A far better idea is to develop your social life away from places in which alcohol holds centre stage. There are boot camps operating in parks in most UK cities these days, gym memberships cost a fraction of the amount of money it takes to drink every day, and failing that, it's completely free to ask a neighbour or fellow parent from the school gates to join you on a teatime jog. Incidentally, reaching out to relative strangers in this way may frighten you to death initially, but you'll be amazed at how good you become at doing it after barely any time whatsoever, and it has the added advantage of building confidence.

When you surround yourself with heavy drinkers who ostensibly treat their alcohol misuse as a great big barrel of laughs, it is exceptionally easy to play down your own booze issues. Conversely, when you spend time with people who value their health above most other things, this too begins to rub off on you. It's a little bit like the difference between a school where the culture is rooted in the clever-people-are-boring-geeks camp and one where it's in the clever-people-are-cool-and-go-places-in-life camp. We tend to be influenced by the dominant mode of thinking, and if you immerse yourself in a bunch of positive-minded, physically robust go-getters, their outlook will almost certainly affect yours to a degree.

Lots of people, when they first embark upon the alcohol-free path, fall into the trap of not going out at all. Fearful of falling off the wagon due to being unable to resist temptation, they choose to stay alone, indoors and away from all possible links to alcohol.

As covered in earlier chapters of the book, this can also be as a result of low confidence and poor self-esteem, but hiding away from new people and situations merely exacerbates the situation and halts progress. Throwing oneself into unchartered territory has the opposite effect: it restores confidence and helps build self-esteem.

I'm not as fit as I would like to be. I still feel a slight sense of dread just before I walk into a tough gym class, and, despite being in the best shape I've ever been in, it's not unheard of for me to collapse on the floor in a sweaty ball at the end of one. But I keep going back for more because I love what I get out of physical exertion. I feel strong and healthy, and I enjoy the company of people who look after themselves. I get a kick out of knowing that I can reach physical goals now, at the age of forty, that I couldn't have got anywhere close to when I was in my twenties.

One more big plus point of exercising: it helps you to sleep. When you've pushed yourself hard, especially when you're outdoors, your body demands sleep in order to recover. I often suffered with insomnia when I was drinking alcohol regularly. I'd have no problems in falling asleep, but I would be almost guaranteed to wake up, clammy and full of self-loathing and fear, in the early hours of the following morning. Nowadays, I go to bed when I'm tired. It feels luxurious to stretch out on clean, crisp sheets when my body is aching just enough for me to know it's been properly exercised as it should be. And then I drift off into a deep sleep, rarely waking

until my natural body clock lets me know I should –
usually about seven or eight hours later. (See more
on sleeping when you are sober in the final chapter.)

Being physically active feels natural and correct –
because it is.

L

Love and Relationships, Minus the Booze

There was so much wrong in the ways I behaved with my old loves, but additionally, there was so much wrong in my choices of boyfriends, and in the fact that the vast majority of the time I spent with them was steeped in alcohol. I never perceived any of my actions back then as being flawed in any way, of course, and I firmly believed that the reason I was so perpetually unlucky in love was simply the outcome of my being dealt a bad hand in life.

To date, my track record with the opposite sex has gone something like this: married at the age of twenty-three, acrimonious divorce four years later followed by several years spent desperately seeking a replacement husband. I was then struck by a sudden and surprising ease at both finding my perfect partner and being able to commit myself to a loving, mutually reciprocated and very happy relationship with him.

It probably won't come as a huge shock to learn that my eventual discovery of romantic fulfilment occurred a few years after I stopped drinking. It wasn't an instant phenomenon; I had to get to know myself first, and begin to demonstrate self-respect and compassion towards myself – something I'd never done as an adult. It was only then that I had even a chance of involvement in a relationship that was equal, loving and completely devoid of any messed up insecurities, manipulation or needy behaviours – things that always, inevitably, drive a wedge through the very heart of our love affairs.

All of the difficulties I faced in my previous relationships were born out of the fact that I had crushingly low self-esteem. I was mistrustful (who would really want to be with me?) and suspicious, which together led to a rotten, destructive belief that whomever I was with at the time would almost certainly be on course to leave me at some point. Consequently, this would drive me to committing acts of self-sabotage. I determinedly pushed several of my partners away, forcing them to the absolute limits of their patience and understanding. Their (almost guaranteed) departure would then provide me with ample evidence that I had indeed been correct that they were never planning on hanging around – a self-fulfilling prophecy locked, depressingly, on repeat.

I sought a sense of security from all of my past relationships. By involving myself with each of my partners, I was actively seeking outcomes that would make me feel better about myself, and so it wasn't the person with whom I was necessarily falling in love – rather, it was the way he made me feel about myself that I was drawn to. I demanded constant reassurance that I was attractive and loveable – knowledge that I was entirely unable to obtain from within. This alone comprised sufficient reason to be with someone, but I also had a deep hatred of being in my own company. In my twenties, me time was an utterly alien concept, and I would pursue distractions of any sort that involved alcohol and socialising. I was bored almost instantaneously upon being left to my own devices and so would call upon a friend to join me in a trip to the local pub or city centre – always with the lure of meeting The One in the back of my mind.

The single action that would have helped me more than anything else (other than becoming alcohol-free, obviously!) during my post-divorce period would have been to remain unattached for a reasonable length of time. However, I was unable to muster the insight or wisdom to do this, and alcohol had a nasty way of spurring me on in all of my misguided adventures with the opposite sex. My lurching from one ill-suited man to the next, the aim of fixing myself consistently being the prime motivator, resulted in years of unhappiness. And this entrenched lack of satisfaction certainly contributed towards the urge to drink.

As well as my inherent need to feel wanted and loved by someone – anyone – I had no idea about the type of person I was. Ergo, this meant that I had not the first clue about who would be a good match for me. My only likes revolved around alcohol, which obviously amounted to me never attracting people who did not feature it heavily in their own lives. Once more, I was trapped within a self-fulfilling prophecy.

Thirty-something divorcee with major lack of trust, especially in men, but everyone really, seeks bloke who likes to drink a lot, and who doesn't mind being questioned over his every move. Not so interested in other activities except smoking and playing pool. Possesses severe lack of self-worth so any takers must be willing to provide ample reassurance in an effort to convince her she isn't all that bad. Must be prepared to be dropped like a hot potato if someone better comes along at any point...

Not terribly appealing, is it?

So what, then, has turned things around for me so drastically that, after a decade and a half of relationship misery, I am finally in a position to enjoy a calm, happy and equal partnership with someone whom I'm in love with and who loves me back? Is it down to luck?

No. It's the result of a chain reaction of events and circumstances that began with the act of me choosing to quit drinking alcohol.

When I quit the booze, I allowed myself an opportunity to find out more about who I am – not how I act after downing two bottles of wine (loudmouthed idiot), but the person I am when I am just being me, unadulterated, untainted and unpolluted. As soon as I began to acquire self-esteem and a basic level of confidence, I stopped being so dependent upon others to boost my feelings of self-worth. I was able to do that myself, which – surprise, surprise – then freed me up to think a little bit more about others. I found myself able to empathise and put other people's needs before my own, a miracle for me after an entire adulthood of pretty narcissistic behaviour.

And while I did still want a loving relationship, it stopped being the main focus of my life. My own and my children's happiness became far more important to me, and I appreciated that even if I did meet the love of my life, there was only me who could make me happy at the end of the day.

Making it happen for you – love, sober

For those already in a relationship, now is a time when you will almost certainly experience changes as you undergo metamorphosis from a dependent drinker into an emotionally mature grown-up. Talk to your partner about how you feel with regard to alcohol and your sobriety, and let them know that you may not emerge as exactly the same person you were when you initially fell in love with her or him. When you become alcohol-free, your perception of the world inevitably alters, and the way you interact with people will similarly undergo changes. It's almost a certainty that when a person drinks heavily and frequently, their emotional maturity will not be as well developed as it would have been had she or he been a non-drinker. This is because each time an emotion has arisen, she or he has quashed it with alcohol and therefore not dealt with the associated feelings.

Suddenly being subjected to the full range of emotions after years or even decades of drinking them away is a bizarre journey to travel, even if you are alone and not having to think of the impact this may have on another person close to you. But when you are in a relationship, ultimately the ups and downs of your mood will have an effect on your partner, and it's crucial that you obtain their understanding and support to help you through this time.

In the end, you will almost definitely reappear from the whirlwind few months of learning how to live free from alcohol as a stronger and more well-rounded individual. It could mean enduring a few trips and falls along the way before you arrive at that place, but if your partner is prepared for that, it can only be a good thing. If your partner is also prepared to help you over the early hurdles of beating cravings and avoiding any situations in which you are likely to feel overwhelmed by a desire to drink, this will be a massive bonus. You could suggest alternative social events that you can enjoy together where alcohol is not the main focus, and if your partner is especially supportive, maybe they might consider reducing their own consumption to alleviate your initial struggles, at least during the first few weeks.

If you are currently single, beginning afresh and considering dating again (ideally at least several months into your new alcohol-free life), then below are a few pointers that will hopefully help you stay on the right track and, ultimately, meet Mr or Mrs Right.

Your plan of action should start with smothering yourself in huge amounts of love. If you are wondering how on earth to do this, remember the chapter earlier in the book on compassion. Go back and reread it if necessary.

Exercising self-love is simply about being kind to yourself. If you are tired, then make time for an afternoon nap. If you're run ragged from a busy, hectic lifestyle, take an hour out for a hot bath with luxurious bubbles and candles dotted around the bathroom. Treat yourself to a new outfit, or a meal with a friend at your favourite restaurant. Have a day in the spa, doing nothing other than pampering yourself and reading magazines. Leave your phone at home and go for a long walk on a sunny day. Sit in the garden for an entire summer's afternoon with a great book and a jug of icy homemade lemonade. Imagine that you are your best friend and carry out all the loving and kind ways you can think of to show yourself that you care. And repeat all of these things for a good few weeks or months, or until it feels normal and proper to treat yourself so well.

And when you reach that point, *perhaps* it might be time to think about reigniting your love life.

For time-poor grown-ups, meeting people of the opposite sex for the purpose of a relationship is most likely to happen at work or in the pub. And if there is nobody at work who rocks your boat, and you no longer get so sozzled that walking up to a complete stranger and telling him you'd really like to snog his face off is not a viable option (thank God), it might be time to give internet dating a whirl. Personally, for non-drinkers, I think internet dating has numerous benefits, the most obvious being that you have the power to determine, very early on, which potential suitors regard booze as all-important, and which don't. If someone's profile emphasises that drinking is their favourite activity then avoid him or her like the plague – you're only wasting their time, and yours, by pursuing a relationship that is most unlikely to end happily.

During your self-compassion phase, you will hopefully have determined which activities you enjoy now that alcohol is not the main love of your life. Look for profiles that mention similar pastimes to the ones you do regularly, and also be selective about a person's emotional attributes. If you've discovered that, without booze, you are actually a calm, quiet type who prefers nights at home watching films, it's probably unwise to pursue a candidate who describes him or herself as a loud party animal. Don't be afraid of including the fact that you don't drink alcohol in your profile – it could be a major stumbling block if this proves to be an incompatibility, so best to get it out of the way at the start. As mentioned previously, those who matter don't mind, and those who mind don't matter, so be honest from the offset.

When you finally reach the stage where you are planning the first date, a walk in a reasonably busy location is a great idea for those who don't drink alcohol. You will probably find that most people will suggest meeting in a pub for drinks – this is fine if you're fully comfortable with your alcohol-free status, but if you aren't ready to draw attention to it just yet then a walk provides a good alternative. Your surroundings work well as a distraction, and awkward pauses in the conversation are not so magnified because you're busy engaged in walking as opposed to sitting facing each other in close proximity. It's easier to bail out on a walk, should you find yourself on the date from hell – simply work out a shorter route than planned back to your car, say your goodbyes and screech off without looking back. If, conversely, everything is going swimmingly, you can always choose to go on to a café or for something to eat in a restaurant so that you can continue the conversation. And *always* remember to let a friend know who you are meeting, where and when for safety purposes.

The final section of this chapter relates to sex – specifically sober sex. Sex is, for many people, something that only ever occurs when drinking is involved. Furthermore, the entire dating experience quite regularly takes place when both parties are often under the influence of alcohol, and so lots of people are unfamiliar with conducting a new relationship stone cold sober. Personally speaking, I didn't venture into a single relationship between the ages of sixteen and thirty-five which was not based on a foundation of extreme drunkenness. And I know I am not alone.

How, then, does one go about the business of sex

minus the crutch of alcohol, so heavily relied upon for decades when even *with* the numbing properties that booze provides, getting naked only ever happened in the dark and with a hefty amount of self-consciousness?

Well, it's a long and meandering learning curve, and it begins (as is the case with so much of alcohol-free living) with eliminating the bullshit from your life. As human beings we are programmed to have sex with the people we are attracted to and/or in love with – it's nature's way of ensuring we are in a solid relationship if we are to reproduce with our chosen partner. If, sadly, we do not feel any attraction to our partner once the booze no longer features in the relationship, then Houston, we have a problem. Cutting alcohol out of your life demands a high level of scrutiny with regard to many things, and one of the major parts of life you will no longer be able to fake, now that you are sober, is whether or not you fancy your partner. If you do find him or her attractive but are suffering from shyness without the bolstering you've routinely required from alcohol, things are far more positive. You can learn to enjoy sex without alcohol. It may feel utterly weird at first (I guarantee it will), but like with so much in life, once you practise a little, it becomes far less awkward.

You can help yourself by shipping the kids off to their grandparents' house, enjoying a romantic evening together and lighting a few candles in the bedroom (no longer the fire hazard it might once have been after large quantities of alcohol). Invest in some flattering underwear, and remove any anxiety by agreeing beforehand that things don't necessarily have to conclude with intercourse. First and foremost, sober sex should just be about loving each other, not diving headlong into bonking one another's brains out – unless you especially want to, of course.

Feeling totally comfortable with being naked and having sober sex will take a while, but it *will* happen if you're both patient. Time has a habit of normalising things, and as long as you don't feel pressured (either from yourself or from your partner), then you should be able to enjoy the process of transforming the act of sex from something that only happened when both of you were half-drunk and unable to remember it properly into sensual, intimate love-making between two people who are truly present in the moment.

When you remove alcohol from the equation and are, as a result, more in tune with your reality, you will find that your relationships with those you love will improve dramatically. Becoming more self-aware, and without the mind-bending properties of excessive alcohol consumption creating a fog around your thought processes, you will be free to feel the full impact of love. Enjoy it – this is one of the most exciting and pleasurable consequences of living an alcohol-free life.

M

Mindfulness

Mindfulness is about love and loving life. When you cultivate this love, it gives you clarity and compassion for life, and your actions happen in accordance with that.
Jon Kabat-Zinn

Mindfulness, originating from ancient eastern meditation practices, has become a much talked about concept during recent years in the West, with this popular movement being initiated by Jon Kabat-Zinn. Kabat-Zinn, Professor of Medicine Emeritus at the University of Massachusetts Medicine School, studied with Buddhist teachers before setting up the Stress Reduction Clinic and the Center for Mindfulness in Medicine, Health Care, and Society. Mindfulness has been extensively studied and proven to be highly effective as a means of managing stress and fostering a sense of calm and wellbeing. It has also been found to help those struggling to beat addictions.

A few months into my new life without alcohol, I felt increasingly aware of the fact that my mind seemed to be permanently unsettled. I found it difficult to sit at peace with my thoughts, and was anxious for much of the time. Inside my head, it felt like a jumbled, churning mass of ideas and worries, like a washing machine on an endless spin cycle. I recognised that this had probably been one of the major motivators in my old drinking habits, that the alcohol had ameliorated this agitated cognitive activity and helped me to relax, but then it had also brought with it a multitude of negative consequences and was a 'solution' I would never contemplate returning to. I therefore opted to employ an alternative far healthier method for calming my mind: meditation.

At the time I knew nothing more about Buddhism and meditation than that which I had gleaned from an old school friend whose dad was a hippy (or so we labelled him in our ignorant youth) who smoked pot while sitting cross-legged in the basement, chanting. Back then, Buddhism, and anything that involved spirituality, was seriously uncool and something I wanted no part of – of course, I knew nothing about the subject and thus was basing my judgement on misconceptions and stereotypes.

At some point along the meandering road that unfurled during my twenties and early thirties, I developed a mild interest in Buddhism. I have mostly been a vegetarian since the age of nine (excluding a brief interlude post-divorce when virtually *all* of my principles and beliefs dissipated, replaced only with a deep affection for wine and cigarettes), and have always been a serious lover of animals, so the

Buddhist value of respecting all living creatures resonated deeply with me. A growing sense of being an integral element of the wider universe began to push me closer still to investigating the Buddhist way of life, and when I eventually stopped drinking at the age of thirty-five, it all seemed to fall into place. I needed to know who I was, to be at peace with myself and, crucially, to establish effective strategies for better managing my life and my thoughts. Buddhism was shouting out to me to dive in and explore further, and so I did.

The founder of the Buddhist religion was called Shakyamuni Buddha, but there are many people who have become, and who will become in the future, Buddhas. The word *Buddha* means awakened one, and refers to someone who is devoid of all flaws and mental obstructions. The original Buddha, born in 624 BC, was a prince who chose to abandon his royal privileges in order to attain full enlightenment through the practice of meditation. For six years, he focused on achieving this aim until finally, beneath the Bodhi Tree and concentrating fully on the Dharmakaya (the essence of the universe, beyond existence or nonexistence, from which all phenomena emanate), he became a fully enlightened being.

Following his own enlightenment, Shakyamuni Buddha proceeded to educate others about finding liberation through the inner development of peace and happiness. His teachings gathered momentum and soon began to flourish throughout Asia. In recent years Buddhism has begun to grow in popularity as a way of life in the West, too.

The core of the Buddhist tradition lies in understanding the mind. It revolves around the theory that we cannot ever achieve happiness via external possessions or surroundings; a bigger house, a new pair of shoes or moving to a different country, for example, are all unable to bring us true and lasting contentment if the mind is not at peace. Meditation is the key for realising this awakening of the mind, the ability to purify and control our thoughts, and it is the practice of Buddhadharma (i.e. Buddhism) that will enable us to achieve this.

The Buddhist tradition highlights unpeaceful states of mind as being the basis of all human suffering. Rather than events themselves being responsible for our anguish, it is the emotional states that erupt as a result of them that bring about unhappiness. Anger and jealousy are examples of unpeaceful states of mind, and the Buddha referred to such states as delusions. It is believed that these delusions can be eradicated through practising Buddhadharma, a highly powerful tool allowing those who master it to be fully in control of their minds.

In order to obtain a state of 'nirvana', the Buddha emphasised the importance of meditation. It is through meditation that we are able to clear our minds and prevent external distractions from disrupting a desired sense of calm. And when we adopt a regular meditation practice, it aids the integration of mindfulness within our daily lives.

Mindfulness has been most helpful for me because

I am something of a worrier. Or, at least, I used to be. I frequently felt as though my stomach was in knots, and the anxiety I experienced over the most innocuous of situations was, at times, debilitating.

When I was at university in my late teens, I was required to present a project to my Media Studies class – basically, I had to prepare a few slides, stand in front of twenty-odd people for ten minutes and share my ideas with them. I was virtually bedridden by the ensuing panic that enveloped me upon being delivered this task by my tutor. I couldn't eat (not that I ate much anyway in those days), I felt engulfed by waves of agoraphobia and I thought of little else for the days preceding the event. In the end, I visited my tutor in private and explained to him that, owing to my eating disorder and associated self-esteem problems, I could no more carry out this presentation than scale the north face of the Eiger. He was sympathetic and allowed me to submit a replacement written assignment, which was good of him but maybe not what I needed at the time. (I've since come to realise that facing one's fears is by far the best way of overcoming them.)

When I consider the person I was before I engaged in a regular meditation practice and simultaneously introduced mindful living into my existence, I am stunned by the fact that I was able to function *at all*. My head was a whirlwind and my emotions ruled the roost; I was a product of Buddhist delusions and had absolutely no idea that there was any other way to live.

To incorporate a meditation practice into one's

daily life takes some initial work and dedication. In the beginning, it's hard. It feels very unnatural to attempt to filter the maelstrom of thoughts that govern the mind when previously it has been allowed to operate in an untrained manner. Imagine this unkempt headspace to be like a stormy ocean with waves battering and pummelling against each other, competing for dominance, and beneath this turmoil, a discomposed mass of churned up water. It will inevitably demand a degree of effort to instil some calm and order.

There is a wealth of information nowadays surrounding meditation and mindfulness which you can locate online, at your local Buddhist centre or in one of the many books that have been written on the topic. I initially got to grips with meditation at the Buddhist centre near to where I live, although I only attended a handful of classes before finding my feet and feeling sufficiently confident to get on with it alone. Occasionally I revisit the centre as a means of gaining more knowledge and improving my practice, but I also do this by reading about Buddhism. And I have discovered that once you master the basics, it becomes increasingly easy and natural to fit meditation into your life.

Through meditating regularly, the mind becomes more manageable, and we are better able to recognise our thoughts as being like clouds passing by. Our thoughts do not define us, and we can opt to ignore them should we choose. The delusions that Buddhism highlights can be conquered once we have the capacity to control our thought processes; what may appear to be insurmountable to a non-mindful person becomes merely an optional cogitation to those who are able to master their minds through meditation practice.

Mindful living is also deeply connected to love and compassion for the self and the people around us, and also for the world and universe at large. When we are not living mindfully, we are missing out on so much and are rendered completely unable to absorb the nuances in people's behaviour that afford us empathy and care for them. And guess what? When you drink lots of alcohol, it becomes virtually impossible to live in a mindful way.

As a drinker, my mind was almost permanently preoccupied with thoughts about alcohol – I was either regretting the way I'd acted the night before when I had been drunk, or I was planning when would be an acceptable time to open a bottle of wine, or whether or not I should walk to the shop for a second. If it was none of these things, then I was probably nursing a terrible hangover and worrying about the physical harm I had, yet again, subjected my body to by consuming so much alcohol. And by allowing these thoughts to gain such prominence, I left no room whatsoever in which to contemplate the present.

I missed a multitude of beautiful moments as an alcohol dependent person. There were the incredible sunrises that I never saw because I was lying, semi-comatose, in my bed, suffering the toxic aftershock of heavy drinking sessions; I failed to capture numerous landmark moments in my elder daughter's childhood that should have been imprinted upon my mind and remained there until my death; I missed the silence of a forest's breath and the feeling of loving another person with my whole heart. The sound of birds singing at first light escaped me, as did the silvery ethereal beauty of countless full moons, suspended in the night sky as I was held captive in an alcohol-induced parallel universe. For me, the expression 'a natural high' amounted to nonsense before I quit drinking. I had no appreciation of the depth of the human experience, the unbelievable joy that we are capable of feeling when we witness a sight or sound that crystallises in our minds owing to its sheer naturally occurring beauty.

When we become mindful in our approach to life we are able to notice all of the wonder of our environment and appreciate it fully. Things stop slipping away from us and instead become woven into the fabric of our souls. And it is this effect of mindfulness that allows us to be at one with the world around us. As the Vietnamese Buddhist monk and teacher Thich Nhat Hanh states:

When you look at the sun during your walking meditation, the mindfulness of the body helps you to see that the sun is in you; without the sun there is no life at all and suddenly you get in touch with the sun in a different way.

Becoming mindful of my existence is, for me, the greatest gift that not drinking alcohol has delivered. It has allowed me to discover the meaning of my own life and of the human experience at large, which finally makes sense to me. Mindfulness has provided me with a strategy for coping with adversity, and for settling a restless mind. It has helped me to sleep better, and to have fulfilling relationships and friendships that I could never have enjoyed in my past drinking life. It has paved the way for learning and understanding my environment, and has propelled me to new places that have helped further my personal growth and development. Mindful living has created a nicer, kinder person in me; one I am proud of. It has presented me with a way of life that is content and in which I am at peace.

Of all the areas I have covered in this book, which together represent the tools and knowledge I have utilised in order to become and stay happily sober, mindfulness is the one I would emphasise as the most useful to you. If you take nothing from the book other than an intention to incorporate the Buddhist practice of meditation into your life, then you will have benefitted greatly from reading it.

Getting started

In order to meditate, it isn't necessary to sit in the traditional cross-legged position, although this is fine if you prefer. Find a comfortable way to sit, on the floor or in a chair, but be sure to keep your back straight in order to prevent sleepiness from setting in (meditation can cause you to feel very relaxed). Close your eyes gently and begin to inhale and exhale naturally through the nostrils with your attention turned fully to each breath. The action of breathing should now be utilised as the focus of your meditation practice.

Think of the mind as a stormy sea , and recognise that the mind will require some time in order to become calm. Different thoughts are bound to enter your headspace and you will probably find yourself concentrating on some or all of them to begin with. When this happens, merely return your focus to the action of your breathing – in, and out; in, and out – until the thought has drifted off and your mind is clear once more. As you breathe, imagine the stormy waters calming and slowly transforming into a tranquil, gentle aquamarine sea, softly lapping the seashore. Align your breathing with each rolling wave and let it wash softly over the beach before allowing it to retreat peacefully back towards the wider ocean.

This breathing meditation is a preliminary form of the practice, but it is a very effective method of stress relief and of increasing your awareness and control of the mind. Try to meditate every morning first thing and gradually increase the duration of your practice. It should become easier each time to bring your mind to a state of calm and inner peace.

N

Nourishment

Perhaps even longer in duration than my battle with alcohol was the one I endured over decades with food. At times this was brutal and combative, and at others the struggle waned somewhat, reduced to merely a vague feeling of weariness and semi-defeat with regard to eating and my calorie intake, but from the age of twelve up until recently, I had a consistently serious fear of weight gain and an ongoing dissatisfaction with my body.

For me, alcohol consumption and my unhealthy relationship with food were always inextricably linked – interwoven mental health issues most definitely cut from an identical ragged cloth. The 'fuck it' button I hit whenever I reached for a bottle of wine in the supermarket (after promising myself I wouldn't drink on a particular night) was the same as when I gorged on half a packet of biscuits or ate an entire giant-sized bar of chocolate in next to no time (when I was allegedly on a 'diet'). The pacts I'd make with myself to remain sober or to stay slim were routinely broken – so frequently, in fact, that they were usually rendered completely redundant at the very point of their creation. For almost twenty-five years – a quarter of a century – I considered food to be the enemy: something I couldn't resist, but which was guaranteed to initiate feelings of utter self-loathing whenever I inevitably caved in and ate.

And it was exactly the same story with alcohol.

When I quit drinking, the negativity surrounding food didn't immediately disappear along with the alcohol. Rather, it was a one-step-forwards-and-two-steps-back scenario where eating was concerned. However, I have finally reached a stage where I've discovered how to manage my relationship with food in a non-obsessive manner. I'm no longer frightened to eat and I understand the connection between my emotions and food a whole lot better than at any previous time in my life.

I never had any problems with my weight as a child; I don't remember considering my body for any reason whatsoever, and I certainly had no self-esteem or confidence issues to contend with. The status quo began to be disturbed as the onslaught of puberty crept ever closer, and I do recall feeling uncomfortable about the imminent transition from child to woman. I found it difficult to accept the arrival of my menstrual cycle, and was mortified when it emerged that I was fairly well endowed in the chest area. A desire to blend into the background, where I could be inconspicuous and small, began to grow within, and it was at this point when food became baneful.

As I matured into my mid-teens, the foundations were laid for what was to become a two-decade long chapter during which I abused my body. I began to deny myself food completely on a regular basis, and by the time I reached seventeen, I weighed around six stone – a three-stone drop from just a couple of years earlier. And I still believed myself to be fat, so terrified of getting any bigger that food became something to avoid at all costs. Lunch comprised of a low fat hot chocolate, dinner amounted to the glacé cherry floating on the surface of a vodka, lime and soda – you get the picture.

As the years went on and I resolutely committed to maintaining my stick thin figure, a disconnection unfolded between myself and my body. The punishing regime of virtually no sustenance together with the alcohol and other drugs I was regularly consuming somehow enabled me to lose touch with my physical self. I seemed to inhabit my head only, while the rest of me shrank and withered and was left to rot. I hated my body, and the desire to force it to cope with unending strain and damage was both strong and perpetual.

The eating disorder became more manageable after the discovery that I was pregnant with my elder daughter at the age of twenty-two. I could no more continue to starve myself than I could smoke, knowing that inside my womb was a new life, utterly dependent on my choices for its survival and wellbeing. My weight crept up, the drugs, booze and cigarettes were abruptly discarded, and for a few years everything felt calm and secure. But old habits die hard, and when my then-husband and I divorced at the age of twenty-seven, the shit certainly hit the fan. All of my dormant coping mechanisms emerged from the woodwork, one by one and as predictably as the sun's rising.

At the age of thirty-five, as a reasonably novice non-drinker just a few months into my sobriety, I became pregnant for a second time. My life was beginning to come together, and the single act of not consuming alcohol had impacted massively on my mental health in a very positive way. By this stage, and for the first time ever in adulthood, I felt as though I was gaining in life rather than losing. Relationships were easier to manage and finally I had a modicum of self-respect. And yet, at the back of my mind, there were still the same niggling anxieties surrounding weight gain that had plagued me since my early teens.

Was it all down to poor self-esteem? Did I genuinely believe that I did not deserve to eat? Or was there something bigger going on, something more convoluted?

People who suffer from eating disorders often fall under the banner of 'perfectionist'. The compulsion to control food intake in such an obsessive manner usually stems from a feeling of being out of control in other areas of life; the anorexia or bulimia is not so much about the food, but rather about exercising discipline and excessive restraint. And the obsessive controlling brings about a sense of comfort and security. Living with an eating disorder also greatly affects how one perceives one's body – the gap widens between a person's soul and the vehicle which houses it and gradually an absolute disassociation between the mental and physical states arises. As a side effect of this, it frequently becomes standard to disregard the body in terms of any other type of self-harming activity, such as alcohol misuse.

When I was drinking a lot, I did not care at all about the consequential damage I was inflicting upon my liver, or the increasing risk I was subjecting myself to in terms of cancer and early onset dementia. Quite the contrary – I wanted to hurt myself; I believed I deserved it. I felt worthless, and the downward spiral of vicious hurt and self-harm brought me a comforting feeling of familiarity. If you are at the bottom then you cannot drop any further. There's a sense of ease to be derived from that knowledge.

When I looked at myself in the mirror I saw only the imperfections: the Caesarean scar; the stretch marks; the too-short legs; the cellulite-ridden thighs; the conspicuous veins. I still tried valiantly to adhere to a calorie intake that would result in a reduction in my weight, but invariably I would lose control, eat chocolate and pizza and drink fatty, creamy coffee drinks, and then I would despise myself all over again in the morning when I stood on the scales.

This was all playing out in my early years of not drinking – I could live with not being a size eight, but I wanted to be thinner. I couldn't escape from the tired old trap of overeating, hating myself, skipping meals, overeating, and on and on. I wanted to believe that it didn't matter – what I weighed and how I looked – but I couldn't.

As the alcohol-free months added up, I found that

most of the aspects of my internal misery over the years were being eradicated. I didn't feel anywhere near so depressed, and the panic attacks from which I had once suffered vanished without a trace. I felt confident and worthy of being here on the planet, and I recognised that I have unique and valid qualities just like everyone else. I also acknowledged that if I didn't work out a way of extracting myself from the circle of madness that formed the basis of my relationship with food then I'd never be truly happy and content.

My belief in *me* as a human being, purely acquired through my ongoing commitment to an alcohol-free life, had the slow but steady effect of making me crave a healthy body. Once I'd worked through the early phase of quitting drinking, it felt like time to repair all the hurt and damage I'd inflicted upon my body over the years, and I finally got a handle on the fact that our mental and physical states are inextricably connected. When we feel good in our physicality, it has a direct impact upon our mental condition – and vice versa. When this penny dropped, I felt able to tackle the food problem, something I'd never been able to do since the closing of my childhood.

This chapter is dedicated to my lovely big sister, who has always had a head for science and common sense, unlike me. I am a little more prone to dreaming and flying by the seat of my pants. For a long time she has been spouting the virtues of various apps to download on to my mobile which would, she assured me, make my life immeasurably easier. To her recommendations, I routinely retorted, 'I haven't got time for that rubbish!' before struggling on with whatever struggles I'd been struggling with. But then I did download one of them – a fitness app. And for the first time in my whole life I felt equipped with the knowledge I had been lacking with regard to the food I should be eating and how best to manage my weight.

It turns out this is not a game of luck where pounds may be shed if the wind is blowing in the right direction, but that actually you can determine body weight by arming yourself with a few facts and approaching the issue with a little bit of canniness. With knowledge comes power, and that power brings an end to fear and anxiety. It's good to eat healthy food, and it's good to exercise, and when you do both it makes you feel happier and healthier inside. And this has a positive effect on your mind, which in turn means that you feel more optimistic and generally better about yourself and your life. This then motivates you further to stay in good physical shape. Life becomes worth living, and to enjoy it fully, you need to take care of your whole self.

Soberistas is awash with concerns over weight loss and questions pertaining to why stones haven't melted off now that people have ditched the booze, and how to ensure they don't consume biscuits with the fervour of a person who hasn't eaten for days. And within the blogs and comments about weight, I often identify that same lack of power and control with regard to food that I had always suffered from. I have realised through trial and error (and with the help and direction of my sensible sister) that in order to enact any major changes in the way you eat and, more importantly, in the way you regard food, it is of fundamental importance to get clued up, emboldening your efforts in any useful way you can think of. And after going down the fitness app route, I would highly recommend getting one of these on your phone to help you out.

Lots of people will advise you that concerning yourself too much with diet and weight loss in the early stages of your alcohol-free life will overload your head with worry and unnecessary additional stress. I would agree with this to a degree – aiming to shed the pounds and fretting about reaching a certain goal weight is not ideal and will only distract from the most important aim of this chapter in your life, which is to recover from an alcohol dependency, *but* adopting a healthy approach to food and exercise is not obsessive. It's not too much and, crucially, it should be viewed as one of the stepping-stones to self-compassion. By thinking about and behaving mindfully towards the food we are consuming, we are showing our bodies the respect and love they deserve. I see healthy eating as the polar opposite to my drinking days. Rather than pouring toxins down my neck, smoking and gorging on food that provided me with no nutritional value whatsoever, now I give my body what it wants in terms of vitamins and nutrients, drink plenty of water and go to bed at a reasonable time – and I feel much more positive as a result.

So many of us wind up engaged in longstanding

and destructive battles with ourselves which are manifested in eating disorders, alcohol misuse and other means of self-harming, and the same core drivers are at the heart of them all. They are born out of (and then aggravated by) an innate separation between the mind and the body, and while we are locked in these behaviours we haven't a hope of being content and fulfilled.

Contentment and the phenomenon of truly liking ourselves occur when we show ourselves respect, and when we listen to what our bodies are asking from us. Mindfulness, as discussed in the last chapter, allows us to focus on what we put into our bodies as opposed to merely eating for eating's sake without paying any attention to the food we are consuming. It becomes a habit, being concerned about treating our whole self correctly, and it's a habit which then extends across all areas of our lives. Consuming entire packets of biscuits and then hating ourselves afterwards is so close to the act of drinking ourselves into oblivion before the inevitable onslaught of self-loathing the following day. It's difficult to move on from either until we adopt a completely new mind-set.

Stopping drinking presents the perfect opportunity to say goodbye to old negative habits and introduce kinder, more compassionate ones – beginning with a good, healthful diet. Download a fitness app, count your steps, eat more vegetables and take pride in your body once again. Reconnect with it – and remember that your physical-self influences your mind. Food is good; it's nourishment.

O

Organise Your Life

When you initially put down the bottle, time can (and probably will) suddenly yawn open before your blinking eyes like a vast desert. You could well be a little disarmed by this in the first instance, experiencing feelings of being lost and adrift, uncertain of exactly what to do with all these novel hours of nothingness. I did not enjoy being cut loose in this manner when I quit drinking. I'm far too busy a person and have never found it easy to relax (minus a bottle or two of wine close to hand), and therefore I grew very bored, very quickly. I believe that of all the triggers that may push a person back into a drinking life, boredom is the one that is most likely to wreak carnage among their beautifully laid plans of sobriety.

The key to dealing with this potential landmine is to get organised. And I'm not talking about rearranging the sock drawer (although even this is better than sitting, twiddling our thumbs and looking longingly out of the window as we contemplate a speedy trip to our nearest purveyor of booze). No, I'm referring to an overhaul, a massive rethink, fitting all sorts of new and exciting things into our lives that previously, when slumped in an alcohol-induced comatose state on the settee, we would never have found time nor inclination for.

When I regard my old life, the one that featured excessive drinking on most days, I honestly cannot fathom how I managed to achieve *anything*. I would leave everything at the drop of a hat if a friend or boyfriend suggested a trip to the local pub and I happened to be childfree at the time. Food shopping got put on hold, and forget cleaning the house or sorting out any administration from my daughter's school. I wouldn't be taking the dog for a walk or doing any exercise. Hobbies of any sort that didn't involve drinking were a no-go, as was helping out a neighbour, cleaning the car, applying for a new job because I hated the one I had, gardening, reading or doing anything! It is a small miracle that I wasn't living in abject squalor and surviving on baked beans.

I must have squeezed a few necessary chores in between my busy social (read: drinking) life, but 'squeezed' is the operative word here. I was literally rushing around doing the bare minimum in order to free myself up for yet another heavy boozing session. I lived to drink, and the rest of my life was a necessary evil that I begrudgingly got on with whenever I had a rare spare moment.

For those of us who have drunk frequently and to excess, life should undergo a huge transformation when the alcohol is removed. If we intend to stick to our aim of not drinking on a permanent basis then we will need to make some pretty significant changes to how we operate. This chapter is about how to work out what to do with our lives now that we're grownups who don't drink.

Get some paper and make a few notes here, and try to be brutally honest. Stopping drinking is an ideal opportunity to radically change the things you dislike about your life and simultaneously introduce lots of positive new activities and people into it. But to get there, you need to be straight up with yourself. It's best to answer these questions when you are a few weeks into sobriety; that way you'll have had a chance to find out a bit more about the type of person you are and what makes you tick.

What sort of person are you – quiet, academic, busy, social butterfly?

Now that you're no longer walloping back the booze at every given chance, you should be able to ascertain with more accuracy what sort of person you are. I always thought I was the life and soul of the party, but since quitting drinking, I've discovered that I'm much happier in the company of just a couple of close friends and usually shy away from larger groups.

Before you can work out what type of things you will enjoy doing, it is important to decide whether you enjoy learning, socialising, being outdoors, indoors, in the company of a lot of people or if you're reasonably solitary. Are you adventurous or cautious? Quiz yourself and write down a good summary of your personal attributes. This is a useful starting point for the following questions.

Do you enjoy being by yourself? Here are some ideas for self-care:

Being alone and enjoying one's own company can take some getting used to as a newly non-drinking person. Many people drink to alleviate loneliness, and it's not uncommon to feel very lonely even when in a relationship, using alcohol to numb the associated emotional misery of being stuck with the wrong person. Being sober and by yourself will probably feel slightly alien initially, but it helps build resilience and confidence because it enables you to find out that you don't always need other people to lean on.

Here are a few ideas for ways to enjoy a pleasant evening in (sober) on your own:

- Meditation is a great start to an evening spent alone; it calms the mind and can spark creativity, which is brilliant if you've recently developed an interest in an arts-based activity – you can do some of that afterwards;

- Putting on uplifting music can really help raise your mood, and watching a film is wonderful when you're not drinking alcohol because, hey, you can remember it all in the morning;

- Spend some money on a few luxurious pampering treats and indulge in a hot, bubbly bath with candles dotted around the bathroom;

- Eat some delicious healthy food, and then spend some time working on a plan of action for creating the life that you really want and deserve;

- Curl up on the settee in your favourite pyjamas with a good book and a few squares of proper chocolate;

- Research on the internet for local classes or groups that might be of interest.

Can you identify emotional issues that might need addressing?

Without alcohol numbing your emotions, are you now able to identify any issues that you routinely struggle with? Are your relationships always ruined as a result of your insecurities and inability to trust? Have you suffered a bereavement or been through a divorce that you feel is still dragging you down? Are you often depressed, unable to feel positive or enthusiastic about life?

Alcohol is utilised by lots of people to mask a wide range of emotional issues. When you remove it, those problems will most likely rise to the surface and knock you sideways. Try not to be frightened by the intensity of your feelings; instead, just accept them as part of the process of learning to live free from alcohol and think about how best to address whatever issues are of concern. Seeing a therapist is a very helpful way to drill down to the root cause of emotional problems – a good therapist or counsellor can help shine a light on confusing and painful matters, and ultimately will set you on a path to wellness. Antidepressants might be worth considering in the short term if you are struggling to hold it together; they can be useful for getting you to a place where you feel strong enough to address the issues behind your depression.

If relationships are often difficult to manage, it may be that time alone is exactly what you need rather than rushing straight from one partner to the next. Consider promising yourself a six or twelve month period in which you concentrate first and foremost on you. Make self-compassion a priority, and learn who you are without alcohol messing everything up. It is only when you are able to love yourself that you have the ability to love another human being fully.

What hobbies did you enjoy when you were a child?

Drinking is a fabulous way to disrupt all the lovely, positive activities we enjoyed as kids. Before booze comes along, young people are free to love all sorts of pastimes and true friendships without even imagining that a mind-altering substance is just the ticket for making things go with a bang. Personally speaking, I lost interest in writing, playing a musical instrument and cooking when I began to drink – before then I was always creating something in the kitchen, playing my violin or scribbling away in a notebook.

Think back now to what rocked your boat as a child, and think about whether any of it would appeal now. It's a nice way to reconnect with the real you – the person you were before alcohol muddied the waters.

Organising your own and your family's lives can help restore self-worth and rebuild broken bridges

Oh, the guilt attached to heavy drinking! Being alcohol-dependent tends to create a bottomless pit of related negativity, not least being the fact that when we're frequently hitting the booze, we are unable to organise our family life properly. Admin stuff gets side-lined, packed lunch ingredients don't get bought, letters are forgotten about and left un-posted, deadlines are missed and appointments cancelled. And often, our emotional availability is depleted due to hangovers and anxieties surrounding the next drink.

But when you put down the bottle, you'll find that you suddenly have masses of time and energy for all those little jobs that were perennially left undone in your previous drinking life. It feels good to know that you're doing a proper job of caring for the people you love, and as well as making them feel a whole lot happier, you'll be happier, too. Guilt is a corrosive emotion that nibbles away at you and destroys your self-worth. Eradicating that guilt and becoming someone you're proud of is a massive step in restoring familial relations *and* your own self-esteem.

Sorting out your finances can serve as a great motivator for staying sober (think about all the things you could do with that money!)

It's not just the money we spend on alcohol that drains our bank accounts as drinkers, it's all the add-ons like takeaways, internet purchases made when under the influence, taxis, cigarettes (if, like I used to, you regularly end up smoking when drunk) and bad choices regarding loans and credit card offers. Plus, there's the money that we never have in the first place because we fail to reach our full earning potential – when we're always hungover and don't have much self-confidence, it's often the case that we wind up stuck in low paid, unsatisfactory jobs rather than flying high in brilliant careers that we're passionate about.

Having a clear head and putting a stop to the drunken nights out (and in – it can be just as expensive, if not more so, when we have a credit card to hand and we've been knocking back the vino all night) means we can get our finances in order. It allows us to focus on what we really want out of life, including our careers. You may decide to retrain or set up your own business, or simply look elsewhere for a better job than the one you have currently.

It took me a while to begin to adopt sensible spending and saving habits after quitting drinking, but there's no way I could have done this at all prior to becoming alcohol-free.

I used to live absolutely recklessly in all areas of life, but especially when it came to my finances. That fostered within me a real sense of fear and insecurity, and I would lean on other people to bail me out on a regular basis. When you are in charge of your finances, you feel a lot more grown-up. It's a good feeling.

Do you need some new friends and/or a new partner with whom alcohol won't be such a big issue?

When you are in the process of addressing your whole life and wondering how it could be improved, it's inevitable that the people who feature in it will pop up and provide some food for thought. If your best mate happens to be a big drinker who would no more consider a social occasion booze-free than she would run naked down the High Street (unless she happens to be a lover of streaking, in which case ignore this analogy), it may be time to look for a few new friends. Sadly, a large percentage of friendships are based solely upon alcohol when we too are heavy drinkers.

It could be that you choose to stick with the same friends but readjust the activities you do together, so that instead of Saturday night in the bar you meet for coffee and a walk on Sunday afternoon. But it's also good to get on board some chums for whom alcohol isn't such a big deal – people who will suggest and happily go along to alternative events and nights out, such as the theatre or something outdoorsy. This will really help you stay off the sauce too, because it will demonstrate that to have fun, you don't require alcohol. When you discover that, in truth, there are a huge number of plus points to sober socialising, you'll want to do more of it. And it's nice to have someone to do it with.

Could you volunteer for a cause that is close to your heart?

Back to self-worth. Volunteering for a cause that you believe in and really care about will boost your self-esteem and help you to feel good inside. It doesn't have to be a commitment of several days per week; just a few hours here and there will instil within you a sense of purpose and contentment. It's also a brilliant way to meet new people and gain a broader perspective on life.

Volunteering helps people to feel better connected to the community, which in turn boosts emotional wellbeing. It can help combat depression as it promotes a sense of purposefulness in individuals. Where the position involves animals to care for, there are even more mental health benefits – regular contact with animals has been proven to reduce stress and improve overall mood. Giving up your time for free may eventually lead you to a new career – by allowing yourself to try a job out voluntarily, you could well find that you discover your ideal vocation.

There may also be an opportunity to volunteer your time on a more informal basis, such as helping out an elderly neighbour.

Are you interested in local politics?

Fairly soon after becoming a non-drinker, I noticed that I began to care about the world a whole lot more than I had ever done previously. When we're in the pub every night or downing a bottle or two of wine at home, the wider political matters of the day are of little consequence to us. But sober, it's a whole different story. We realise that we can make a difference, participate and have our voices heard, and we are of equal importance to everyone else in society.

With your newfound hours of freedom from booze, you may wish to get involved in local politics. Again, there are huge benefits to be had in terms of making new friends, creating a focus in life away from alcohol, bolstering self-esteem and giving you a sense of purpose.

Laying down a plan and setting out a timeline for achieving the goals will make it easier to get out there and start living without alcohol holding you back. Yes, it will feel as scary as hell to begin with, but try to motor on regardless of your fears. Very quickly you will start to reap the rewards – emotionally, financially and in terms of your personal development.

P

Perhaps I Could Moderate?

No, you can't.

This chapter could well begin and end there, but I'll elaborate a little in order to get the message across properly. Everyone who has struggled with an alcohol dependency and quit drinking then gone on to enjoy a few weeks, or even months, alcohol-free, with all the associated benefits, will at some point probably play out a variant of the following conversation in their head:

'I've done really well; I haven't had a drink for weeks/months/ages!'

'Yes, perhaps you didn't have such a problem after all.'

'You know what? You're right – I do feel as though I've cut myself off a bit by not drinking. I miss being able to go out and have a few drinks with my friends/husband/wife/whoever.'

'You've obviously not got a problem because you've not touched a drop for so long. Go out and let your hair down – you only live once, and anyway, you're an adult. You can do exactly what you want.'

'Sod it, you're right! I'll just go out and not drink

much. I will moderate. I'll only have one or two glasses; it'll be fun.'

To begin with, you are reading this book, which points to the certain conclusion that you *do* have a problem in controlling your alcohol consumption. Even when I was blacking out virtually every week, enduring hangovers every other day and living for the weekends when I could drink myself into oblivion, I *still* had no desire to stop drinking. Around that time, my friend lent me a book about quitting, and upon reading in the first chapter that people who have crossed the invisible line into alcohol dependency territory must stop altogether and drop any notions of moderation, I promptly slammed it shut and refused to read another word. What? I asked myself in abject horror. Is this man for real? Stop drinking alcohol permanently – what the hell would I do with my life? Who would I become? What would be the point of existence? (The fact that I was asking myself these questions at all should have initiated the ringing of major alarm bells, but back then I had two feet plonked doggedly in denial.)

However, *you* have progressed beyond that stage and you are reading this book, which is proof of the fact that you do indeed have a real problem with controlling alcohol – and, happily, you now want to rectify it. So that's the first point to stress on this much-debated topic of moderation.

The second is this: to do anything well in life, one must demonstrate passion and dedication for whatever that 'thing' is. Imagine a mountaineer embarking upon climbing Mount Everest while pondering whether her fellow climbers would be offended if she sparked up a cigarette. Consider a cross-channel swimmer who carries out all the necessary training but sneaks in a few pizzas and burgers here and there among the strict diet to which he is supposed to be adhering, or a dancer who kind of wants to be the principle ballerina in a production but for half of each week chooses to stay in bed all day, watching mindless TV and eating junk food.

Becoming a Soberista – that is to say, a person who does sober really well – is not a part-time job. You can't be half-committed to sobriety; you either do drink, or you do not. For me, the only successful way to stop drinking was to learn to love an alcohol-free life with as much vigour as I had shown so consistently towards drinking. If you are aiming to moderate, then essentially you are still seeing worth in alcohol. You are seeking its inclusion in your world because you believe it to have merit.

Now, for a person who has not struggled to control their alcohol intake and for whom drinking has never been particularly problematic, alcohol may well *have* merit – more than likely, it does. For, as mentioned earlier in the book, drinking allows for a loosening of both the tongue and inhibitions in social situations, and it relaxes us, enabling us to forget more quickly the stresses and strains we all face in life.

But for people who have routinely shown that they cannot stop drinking once they begin; for those who are regularly landing themselves in trouble as a result of consuming alcohol; for alcohol-dependent people who so easily and quickly fall into a state of obsessive thinking and planning surrounding booze – how much? How soon? What would she think if I bought another? – for all of these people (and I include myself in this group) alcohol does not have merit. It simply is not the same substance for us as it is for non-problem drinkers, at least in terms of the effects it wields upon both us, the drinkers, and the people in our lives.

In the years preceding my final decision to stop drinking, I attempted on countless occasions to moderate my consumption. I visited a hypnotherapist and asked that he instil within me the magical 'moderation' switch. I would impose strict rules regarding the category of booze I'd allow myself to drink on a night out – bitter or lager but never wine, owing to the latter being so much stronger in terms of ABV and therefore more likely to cause me to fall over in a drunken heap. I told myself not to drink on Mondays, Tuesdays or Thursdays (but never managed to stick to this regimented structure because inevitably I would experience a bad day and thus 'need' a drink, or it would be someone's birthday and I would 'have' to drink, or a boyfriend and I would split up and I would 'deserve' to drink). I'd venture out for a social event and chastise myself before I'd even started to hit the booze, recalling past misdemeanours and promising not to repeat them in the hope that I would be frightened enough, this time, to be sensible. And, of course, I *would* repeat them because of the third point to make on the issue of moderation: alcohol is a mind-altering substance.

If you're playing around with the notion of moderation in your mind, it will almost certainly be during the times when you're sober, thinking clearly and uninhibited by the effects of ethanol on the brain. The limitations you are setting for your drinking patterns are entirely reasonable and eminently doable, for they are created in reality. The problem with remaining steadfast in your resolve to abide by these rules lies in the fact that alcohol changes how you think, so that what made complete sense to you pre-drinking will happily fly out of the window once you have alcohol in your system. Consuming just one alcoholic drink will harm your prefrontal cortex, the part of the brain that makes decisions and weighs up the pros and cons of a situation. This is the element of your brain that affords you self-control, and drinking numbs it, leaving you devoid of any ability to exercise self-restraint. Physiologically then, drinking alcohol destroys any intention you may have had at the outset to moderate the amount you drink.

Let us remind ourselves too that alcohol is a diuretic. When we set about drinking, we quickly desire to drink more in order to quench our resulting thirst.

Yet another reason to take on board that aiming to moderate really sucks is this: being alcohol-free is a truly lovely, freeing and joyous way to live your life. There are no qualifying components to this statement. It is just the simple truth that when you cannot easily control your alcohol consumption, being sober is bloody brilliant. I can still recall, with a smile, the high that I encountered during the light bulb moment when it dawned upon me that I would never, ever drink again. No more mornings darkened by scant half-memories of the previous night; no more unwanted sexual encounters; no more staring at myself in the mirror with pure hatred in my eyes; no more fear about developing any one of the plethora of alcohol-related diseases and illnesses; no more frittering away all my money when drunk on unnecessary and silly things that I didn't need; no more wondering about who I might be if only I would get my act together and start living.

The energy and time I wasted on thinking about drinking was vast. It occupied certainly half, if not more, of my headspace – the regrets, the fears, the panic attacks, the shame and the debating whether or not I should buy a bottle after promising myself earlier I would not. My thoughts were so dominated by alcohol that it defined me. It was the most considered aspect of my world. And it was exhausting.

Since I stopped drinking, my thoughts are my own; I am completely free to think of matters of gravitas – the things that count and which will have a positive impact on my present and my future. Life as a person who has decided fully to commit to being a non-drinker is simplistic, spacious and unencumbered. It allows for time to think about things other than alcohol, which for me has been priceless.

Alcohol-related thinking is a waste of time – it amounts to being a slave, because that's essentially what the alcohol-dependent person is: a drudge who wakes up and thinks of booze, spends all day worrying and lusting after the stuff, and then finally falls asleep in a drunken haze. And even if your plan to moderate seems to be fairly successful to begin with, there is no doubt that it will demand such effort and thinking time that you may well ask yourself whether it is worth it.

A couple of years after I quit drinking, I was invited to take part in an episode of the ITV programme *Tonight*, focusing on heavy alcohol consumption in the UK. As part of the programme, I underwent a FibroScan, a relatively new test that reveals fibrosis or fatty deposits within the liver. Thankfully, the results showed that I had not inflicted any permanent damage on my liver. After the test, the hepatologist who presented me with its outcome asked me a few questions about my erstwhile alcohol intake, and I shared with him the full story. We discussed my out-of-control drinking patterns and some of the situations I'd ended up in as a result, how I had obsessed about drinking so much, and the loss of self-worth I had suffered after more than two decades of regular binge-drinking.

That lovely physician informed me I had so conclusively crossed the line into alcohol dependency that he was quite certain I would never be able to learn to moderate my intake, and that I had indeed made a very sensible decision in cutting the stuff out of my life for good. Reader, his words were like music to my ears. In recent months I had been toying with the moderation game, weighing up whether or not I was really that bad and if, now that I had been sober for a good length of time, I would be safe to dip a toe back into the murky world of drinking. During my conversation with the doctor, I felt as though I was being yanked back on a tight piece of elastic from a place of utter danger and stupidity to a beautiful and safe haven – the world of contentment and peace which I now inhabit.

To anyone who has persistently demonstrated a lack of ability to control his or her drinking but is debating an attempt to moderate, I would pose this question: what the hell would be so different now? What has changed from the last time you promised yourself that you would 'only have a couple'? Surely the lure of moderation is the devil in disguise, playing one last trick in an effort to suck us back into the desperate cycle of addiction. Let's not forget how easy it is to regard the amount we consume in an ever-diminishing manner in terms of the danger it poses to our mental and physical states. Initially, one bottle of wine per night may appear to be a monumental amount of booze, but drink it for long enough and it becomes the standard. Our bodies will soon begin to demand more in order to achieve the same effects.

A shift in thinking from believing a life of sobriety to be the dullest and most pointless one imaginable to perceiving it as a gift of freedom and positivity is the key to successfully beating the booze. And for those who expressly wish to moderate their alcohol consumption, this goal remains categorically out of reach. The planning and worrying, the fears and self-doubt, are all still lurking within the mind of the moderator – even if they are not getting blind drunk on a regular basis because their excessive restraint is (for the moment, at least) having a limiting effect upon their intake.

A final point to make on moderation is this: it can (and usually does) take a while for the penny to drop that for people who cannot control the amount they drink once alcohol has entered their body, the happiest and easiest way to live is to be alcohol-free. Initially, for lots of people this for ever sobriety can be a frightening concept to grasp, meaning that they require several attempts at moderating before they can finally accept that it is just too damn hard, too exhausting and too perilous to be worth the effort. But each individual failure to moderate can be viewed as a stepping-stone in making it across to that happy place of sobriety – just remember that for some, the river is far wider than it is for others.

Q
Questions on Quitting

If you've reached the stage where you recognise that you and booze have had your fun and now is the time to call it a day, no doubt a multitude of questions will be springing up in your mind. There will be questions being asked *of* you too by friends, family and acquaintances pertaining to why you've suddenly chosen to knock drinking on the head. For the unprepared, these probes into what is often a deeply personal and private matter can be perceived as accusatory and pressurising, and ultimately can lead to a person caving in and drinking.

So much about successful sobriety stems from inner confidence and an unshakeable belief in an alcohol-free life. Particularly, it is derived from the way in which someone considers her or himself to fit into such a life. Alcohol dependency is a very difficult thing to acknowledge, especially when all around you are drinking gallons of booze on a regular basis and seemingly not giving a hoot about their reckless ways. And unless you're the archetypal addict who is so continually drunk that it's impossible to ignore, it's likely that the people around you will be a little taken aback when you announce that from now on, it's the sober road all the way for you.

When you adopt an alcohol-free life, it becomes necessary to relearn much of how you go about your daily existence. It's not merely about ordering a glass of lemonade at the bar as opposed to a large bucket of red wine; it amounts to the reconfiguring of yourself, working out what makes you tick and with whom you wish to spend time. It will inevitably force you out of your comfort zone and into the world of real feelings, raw emotions and all sorts of experiences that previously you've avoided by hiding behind alcohol.

Preparation is key for dealing with questions about your choice to stop drinking, as is the knowledge that the brain *does* have the ability to change due to its neuroplasticity. What you may believe to be fixed is not. When we imagine a scenario playing out enough in our minds (even without doing it in real life), our brains gradually begin to lean towards it as the default. This is incredibly useful for helping you in the face of inquisitions about why you are now sober because you can literally pre-order your natural response by practising it internally. Work out the questions that you suspect may be thrown your way, and then spend time acting out in your mind how you will respond. The more you do this, the more readily you will be able to bat off the inevitable interrogations into your newfound non-drinking status and present the calm demeanour of a confident, alcohol-free person.

Here are a few questions that you may soon face, together with some responses to practise:

Why are you not drinking?

This is the first and most obvious one, and despite its seemingly innocuous and simplistic nature, it has the potential to open up a massive can of worms and make you, the non-drinker, wish to fall through the floor. It constitutes a direct probe into your lifestyle choice and has an invasiveness that you may well be unused to – and rightly so. A person would not usually ask a stranger, 'Why are you not eating any bread today?' at an event where bread was being served. And yet, where alcohol is concerned, a person's decision to rebuff it is commonly perceived as being up for public dissection. This is quite probably due to the fact that most people (certainly in the western world) drink alcohol, and the majority of drinkers hold an opinion about it.

Alcohol is a toxin, which increasingly is being highlighted in the media as a health threat. To drink is to consume a potentially harmful substance knowingly, and often those who do so slip into defence mode should they feel their actions are being challenged. (Smokers regularly act in a similar way whenever they suspect their choice to smoke is under attack.)

I am most definitely the type of person who reacts badly to being given the third degree about any of my personal choices. I don't feel as though I owe anyone an explanation for life issues about which I've made a considered and private decision. However, I am also someone who believes that *not* drinking alcohol can be stigmatised almost as routinely as drinking far too much is, and I feel obliged to help improve this status quo. I'm an activist for the sober life, I suppose one might say, and I enjoy discussing the subject with people for whom the concept of teetotalism is utterly alien in an effort to help them understand things better.

When I was newly sober, however, I would rather have poked myself with a sharp fork than have had a conversation with *anybody* regarding alcohol, and especially my decision to not drink it. Back then, my response would have been emitted as a barely audible, 'Hmm, well, I kind of was drinking too much and I ended up in hospital and now I think it's probably, you know, best if I don't bother with it ...' while shoegazing and hoping to God the enquirer would leave me alone.

My advice for how to deal with this question would be first to ask yourself three things:

- Do I owe this person an explanation about my life choices, and do I really care about their opinion of me?

- Am I comfortable and secure in the reasons as to why I no longer drink, and can I convey these satisfactorily?

- Does this person have a further agenda regarding their question to me, i.e. is she or he a big drinker and therefore feeling threatened by the fact that I'm now sober?

Establish answers to these questions *before* you are ever faced with a person quizzing you on why you're not drinking. How you respond will depend on whom it is you are talking to – your partner, for example, does have a vested interest in your social behaviours and their interest is perfectly legitimate. The half-pissed great uncle bombarding you with intrusive questions at a family wedding, on the other hand, is not someone who particularly needs to know your business, and how you answer his questions would be a totally different kettle of fish.

If you are feeling happy and open to being honest and conversational about why you are now a non-drinker, here are a few simple suggestions for answering the question 'Why are you not drinking?':

- I got to a point in my life where hangovers were so debilitating they were wiping out entire weekends. I just can't handle them like I could when I was younger.

- I care about my health and felt as if alcohol was taking more than it was giving – I'm feeling generally more healthy as a result and have loads more energy.

- I've really got into running / swimming / yoga / any other fitness activity, and drinking was having an impact on it. I suppose I've grown out of it a bit.

- Drinking was starting to happen too frequently and I wanted to get in control of it before it started to control me.

I would avoid using antibiotics or driving as excuses as these are both only viable in the short-term, and ultimately you will feel hampered by having created a lie for explaining your choice not to drink. By using one of the above options instead, you won't be blatantly admitting that you feel as if you've crossed the line with alcohol; you will merely be stating that your life is of value to you and that alcohol was impinging upon it.

Are you an alcoholic?

Ah, the million-dollar question. I've lost count of the number of times I have been asked this, usually by journalists keen to put a salacious twist on their story while separating the responsible drinkers from the addicts. In my experience, the grey area in between the two is one that causes untold discomfort to lots of those who regularly consume alcohol.

Many people find solace in hearing that problem drinkers are in actual fact alcoholics because it neatly etches a line in the sand, demarcating between their own drinking behaviours and those of people who are totally lost to the substance, mired in the dark world of addiction. I do not like the word alcoholic – for me, it's a highly negative label, and one which removes any of an individual's other characteristics. Being referred to in this way effectively categorises her or him as an alcoholic and nothing more; their humanity is forgotten.

Furthermore, there is no test to determine whether a person is an alcoholic or not. Many of the medical definitions of an alcoholic are applicable to people who would never in their wildest dreams define themselves as such – someone who drinks large amounts over a sustained period and has problems in reducing their intake; someone who strongly desires alcohol; someone for whom drinking results in not fulfilling responsibilities and finding themselves in risky situations; someone who experiences physical withdrawal symptoms when they stop and whose tolerance is measured in terms of the amount they are able to consume. It is not deemed necessary for all of these to be present in order for someone to be considered (in medical terms) an alcoholic. Considering this list, I could easily think of a large number of people I know who would fall within the category of alcoholic, and I would bet decent money on none of them agreeing that is what they are.

So, for me, 'alcoholic' is an unhelpful and stigmatising label, and I would never employ it to describe my own relationship with alcohol. This is not denial; it is born out of my wish to be perceived as a human being, equal to all others, and not to be pigeonholed in any way. I am, for the record, fully accepting of the fact that I was once alcohol-dependent and that I will never be able to moderate my consumption. I just have no wish to define myself as an alcoholic.

To this question, then, my answer usually amounts to a succinct version of the above: 'I don't really like the label "alcoholic" as for me it is loaded with negativity. I know that I had a problematic relationship with alcohol, which is what led me to quitting drinking five years ago. Do I have a problematic relationship with alcohol now? No. I don't drink.'

I'm going to the bar – what are you having?

I would advise that you run this scenario through your mind whenever you have a spare minute in the lead up to a night out. Work out what you will ask for, anticipate that your choice of drink could well spark off further questioning, and visualise yourself serenely enjoying a glass of sparkling elderflower pressé/alcohol-free lager/mineral water with ice and lemon/whatever-else-takes-your-fancy-and-does-not-contain-booze. Focus on the positive consequences (of which there are many) of choosing this alcohol-free beverage and zoom in on all of the little details. Picture how you will look, steady on your feet and without heavy eyes or slurring your words; listen to your conversation, interesting and engaging instead of boring and repetitive; see yourself on the morning after, waking up without a dry mouth and make-up

172

streaked down your face (if you wear it), feeling energised and ready to face the day; remind yourself about how good it feels to be fully in control of your choices.

The more you replay this scene in your mind before it takes place in reality, the more naturally it will occur when it actually takes place. Your brain will slip into the default setting that your internal play-acting has created, helping everything to feel normal and easy.

How you choose to answer questions about your decision to quit drinking, and indeed whether you choose to answer them at all, is completely up to you. You may well discover that the people in your life are not that bothered about whether you drink or not, and even if they are, it will only be a passing fancy and something they forget all about soon enough. When it comes down to it, how you react to enquiries into your sobriety will set the tone for how others regard it. The more you can maintain a confident composure, making it clear that you are happy with your life, the more it becomes difficult for others to chastise or mock you for having become alcohol-free.

There is a growing movement in society, I believe, comprised of individuals fed up with alcohol defining their very existence. They want more from life than weekend hangovers and regularly making fools of themselves when drunk. The more open we all are about heavy drinking and/or choosing not to drink alcohol, the less stigma will be attached to both. I see people positively affecting their friends and family in terms of alcohol consumption purely by sharing the fact that they have cut out alcohol and are feeling much better as a result. It's almost an unspoken truth – the unimaginable thought that *not* drinking could well make us happier than drinking. And when we, as non-drinkers, 'come out' and discuss with loved ones our new alcohol-free life and how much we're enjoying it, it can prompt them to consider making changes to how they live.

A word of caution, though: the evangelical convert to sober living is not a model to aspire to. People will only arrive at the decision to quit drinking if and when they are ready. No matter how harmful a person's drinking habits are, it will be impossible to convince them to put the bottle down until they want to. The best way to approach this matter is to lead by example, quietly and assuredly. Being able to inform questioners about why you are no longer drinking in a positive and confident way is a very good place to start.

R

Regrets and Moving On

Do I regret any of my behaviour from the years during which I regularly drank alcohol? Well, the answer is yes and no. Or, to qualify that statement, there are many things that I *have* regretted but have subsequently let go of, a process that has allowed me to move on to enjoy a free state of mind.

I believe it to be a necessary part of healing, post-alcohol dependency, to work through all the stuff we've done when drinking of which we are not especially proud, to acknowledge those things and to focus on why we have acted in particular ways. This helps us to understand ourselves better, which, of course, is the best means of ensuring those same mistakes are not repeated in the future. The practice of self-analysis is important, as is the need for us to accept a degree of personal responsibility; there is nobody else to whom we can attach blame when it comes down to our actions when drunk. Recognising this was, for me, one of the first major steps I took in terms of my alcohol-free personal development.

Having said that, there is nothing to be gained whatsoever from perpetual self-flagellation, continuing for years after our awful drinking misdemeanours have finally ended. Yes, we've all acted stupidly when drunk, and most of us have let people for whom we care and love down. However, when we opt to become alcohol-free, it means we've arrived at a positive point of change, and this deserves credit. Essentially, we are all human beings, and human beings make mistakes.

In the early days of my sobriety, I could barely manage to think for even a moment about certain instances of my erstwhile drunken behaviour. I found it excruciating to relive occasions on which I'd made a total fool of myself in public; the times when I had been with my daughter and obviously under the influence of alcohol; the relationships I had entered into with the wrong people because I had been so out of it that I had no clue what I was getting myself into. I tortured myself with replaying situations in my mind, usually when I was in bed trying to sleep and the world stopped spinning for the first time that day. And my God, I hated myself. There were numerous, seemingly endless nights spent with my face stuffed into the pillow in an attempt to muffle wracking sobs, and days when I couldn't bring myself to leave the house for fear of having to face someone, knowing all that I had done in my murky past. For a very long time, I had absolutely no idea how on earth I would ever move on from those regrets.

I imagine many people think, as I once did, that when you're guilty of drunkenly doing terrible things or speaking harsh words to those you love then you should never be forgiven. The chastising hand of an unseen disapproving entity seemed to follow me around for months – years – reminding me of endless awful situations, berating me and tormenting me for who I had been when alcohol was my closest friend. For a long time, this dark mental trap prevented me from moving away from all the negatives that sat behind my alcohol misuse. It threw up an iron barricade that consistently repelled self-respect in favour of self-hatred.

As is the case with so much of the emotional turbulence that erupts when we quit drinking, resolving these deeply entrenched feelings of guilt and self-hatred is a game of time. There is an upside to this painful period of self-flagellation, which is that it enables us to accept the way things once were, to take responsibility where it should be taken and, crucially, to recognise that we have now changed and no longer act in those same regrettable ways. I view that guilt-ridden phase of my own life as the final dying embers of a fire that represented the old, drinking me; once the last glowing sparks had died away, a rejuvenated and free version of myself was given the chance to emerge.

Observers will routinely cast judgement upon people who drink more than they should and consequently engage in behaviour they wouldn't contemplate when sober. There's an unspoken rule pertaining to alcohol consumption that affords individuals the freedom to drink to a point – to drink until tipsy, but before they fall to the floor; to enjoy alcohol, but not to rely upon it; to suggest going for a 'little drinky-poos', but only when the social environment dictates this to be acceptable. When the invisible boundaries are overstepped, the drinker is usually aware of it, and the sense that others are disapproving becomes palpable. Many people are highly hypocritical when it comes to alcohol consumption. Occasionally someone will drink more than they intended, but because it's a rarity it's laughed off – the same cannot be said for people who regularly down sufficient quantities for it to be seriously mind-altering and damaging.

Picking up that first drink when you are unable to moderate your consumption is, on the surface of it, an irresponsible choice. But when you are caught in the grip of an alcohol dependency, you can *never* accept that just one glass will ultimately lead to you being completely out of control. Whenever the dependent drinker pours an initial drink, it is with the intention and belief that 'this time will be different'. I can count on one hand the instances when I drank in the full knowledge that I would continue until I blacked out. Mostly, I was seeking an indulgent high, a sense of frivolity, a nirvana I hadn't experienced for many years but which I always hoped I would find again each time I drank.

All of this does not amount to an excuse as to why we should blame the booze and not take any personal responsibility for our drunken actions. But I believe it does give us the right to know that the person we are as a regular drinker and the one we transform into when sober are two utterly different embodiments of the same base model. We can separate the two and have faith in the non-drinking version of ourselves, knowing this sober person won't let us down.

Time equates to medicine for the soul. The process of reliving painful situations and hating the very core of who we are is merely a component part of the healing we undergo when we put down the bottle for good. We think it, feel it all over again, blame ourselves, despise ourselves, don't want to leave the house, tell ourselves we're no good, and wonder whether it will ever go away and leave us in peace to repair our broken self. And slowly, as the months pass by and the seasons fade into one another, that sense of shame and self-hatred incrementally slips away, leaving behind a few memories that admittedly do not comprise our proudest moments, but which eventually we are able to accept as a part of our history.

Regret is a funny old thing. All of the many paths that we walk during a lifetime, the people we interact with, fall in love with (and often fall out of love with) and work alongside, the stupid situations we find ourselves in, the amazing experiences we live through, the places we visit where old blinkers are stripped away and new horizons come to the fore – all of these things create us as individuals. Some days will be terrible, many will be fairly bland, and some will feature rare glimmers of ecstasy – moments of pure happiness that stay sharp in our minds for ever. But a major element of the person we are is formed by the bad stuff – the really gut-wrenching events that, as they occur, are impossibly painful to live through. And the entire journey that is alcohol dependency inevitably lays down some of the building bricks of which we are made.

I woke up one morning in my then-boyfriend's bed, alone and with no clue as to his whereabouts. It turned out I'd let myself down again, got steaming drunk and flirted with his friend in front of his face then screamed obscenities at him – par for the course, once upon a time. I lay in the wrinkled sheets in his dark, poky room, a familiar sense of panic and fear over what had happened the previous night rising from my stomach like a cold fog. I didn't move for hours. Eventually he returned and ... well, it wasn't pretty. He was abusive; I thought I deserved it, so I took it and begged him to forgive me. I grabbed him, clinging on for dear life, screaming at him through snotty tears and imagining that without him I'd crumble and become dust.

'What have I done? I love you. I didn't mean it, I was drunk, I drank too much just this once, it was a stupid mistake...'

I bumped into the boyfriend's friend years later on a garage forecourt. God knows what he thought of me – I wanted to tell him I'd changed, that all that stuff was played out by the old me, someone who was now dead and buried. He hugged me and said it was lovely to see me, how was I doing? Where was I living now? Had I seen the boyfriend recently? He was no longer in touch. I put on a veneer, climbed into my car and drove up the road where I pulled over and sat for a while, thinking about that day all those years earlier when I had crawled along the dirt-ridden floor of self-loathing, desperately craving a permanent escape from myself. And I only managed to reconcile the person I was back then with the one I am as a non-drinker because of self-compassion.

What would I make of me as I was then, circa 2005? I was an emotionally overwrought and desperately sad woman who actively despised herself, but mostly did her best to be a good mum. I wanted a 'proper' family – as I saw it then, this meant having a long-term partner to fill the shoes of the ex-husband who'd left me, and I mistakenly used alcohol as a means of lifting myself into what I believed to be an attractive sphere in order to find The One. And so, drunk and damaged, I stumbled into countless wrong relationships that were never going to last, due to me being inherently ill-equipped to love myself, never mind a significant other.

And did this set of circumstances mean that for the rest of my life I should beat myself up?

Well, I made the decision that it did not. Instead, I chose to forgive myself and create a better life cemented in sobriety, one in which I could trust myself not to do the silly, shameful, out-of-character things that once caused other people to judge me harshly and me to avoid looking in mirrors because I hated the person who looked back.

We get one shot at this life. I am staggered by the truth of our existence, not continually, but every so often when the brutality of infinity hits me like a sledgehammer and I am reminded that one day I will be gone for ever. Not sleeping, not resting, but gone for good – an eternal piece of the universe that will never again have the chance to think or speak. And with that awareness comes an acute realisation how monumentally wasteful it would be to spend the days in which I am lucky enough to be alive chastising myself for all of my past mistakes. Much of this thinking is bound up in mindfulness – living in the present and being grateful for every aspect of my daily existence, from the cup of tea I drink first thing to the soft, warm bed I climb into at night.

And furthermore, I like myself today. For many years, I could not have written those words with one ounce of sincerity, but it's a different story now. And if I like the person I've developed into, essentially I have to accept all the things that led to my being. All of the stuff, good and bad, embarrassing and amazing, shameful and beautiful, the moments of pride and the days endured in a state of emotional agony. I must acknowledge that I drank a lot – for a long time alcohol was granted a secure status, residing in the higher echelons of my life, and I was dependent upon it for a fair few things, from social confidence to sexual freedom to perceived happiness and the ability to relax and switch off. I sometimes belittled the negative consequences of my alcohol consumption and the effect it had on those around me. Truthfully I was in denial about the wreckage lying all around me as a direct result of what I was drinking. Messiness, the bad memories and the nasty taste left in my mouth born out of alcohol – all of these things got me to today, to this place that I love.

In the end, when we stop drinking, all those sad regrets are slowly overshadowed by new, positive thoughts about who we are and the life we are now leading. Like the Earth, comprised of sediment and rock, broken down and moulded by the wind and the rain, our old memories are replaced by new layers, one on top of the other. A new foundation settles into permanence, gradually pushing the drinking flashbacks further and further back into the recesses of the mind.

The world can undergo a metamorphosis and become a positive place post drinking, and the version of you inhabiting it will be a very different creature to the one who pinballed between bad decisions when under the influence of alcohol. Most likely, your heavy drinking did not stem from nothingness. It came to fruition because of circumstances and events that shaped you in that way, making you what you were. But when we become alcohol-free, we gain clarity which makes it entirely possible to catch our destinies as they are unfurling and alter the course of where we are heading – should we choose to do so. It requires a solid stance and a commitment to an alcohol-free life to be able to achieve this, but it remains within the grasp of every individual who once hated him or herself and subsequently drank to the point of mental obliteration to cope with those feelings. Inner peace and truly loving the person we are is something we can all attain, but to do so demands living a life of which we are proud.

S

Soberistas

I couldn't write a book about sobriety and not devote a chapter of it to Soberistas, the social network website I set up in 2012. I think Soberistas offers so much to people who are seeking a better, happier and healthier way of living, which crucially does not involve alcohol. I created the site as an online space that I would have wanted to use myself when I first stopped drinking, and this dictated much of the early version of it and how it stands at the time of writing, three and a half years later. Soberistas is not just about stopping drinking; it is an inspirational wellbeing resource that promotes a wholly healthful way of life of which being sober is an integral component.

I'll be honest, when I first quit drinking in 2011, I would not have attended Alcoholics Anonymous meetings. The core reason behind this was I didn't particularly fancy labelling myself as an alcoholic – I wasn't really sure what one was or whether I was one. I also had a hunch that I wouldn't be able to gel with the religious overtones of AA; I felt that my successful sober life would be found in the restoration of my self-belief through overhauling my life rather than following any particular prescriptive method.

Soberistas was born out of an accumulation of the above. I strongly believed in the need for a safe, non-judgemental online space where people in the depths of despair because of their relationship with alcohol could log on, around the clock, and speak to others who could completely understand their problems, wouldn't judge and could offer advice and hope for a better future.

When I look back on the embryonic phase of Soberistas, I'm so pleased that somehow, despite having chronically low self-esteem at the time, I decided to aim high with my new website rather than follow the aim low strategy I had characteristically favoured previously. This stemmed from my inherent belief in Soberistas right from the start – it struck me as the perfect way to help people who were in a similar predicament to me because of their inability to control how much alcohol they drank. It made sense, and I knew it would help people.

On a very basic level, Soberistas offers the same type of help as Alcoholics Anonymous in that it is made up of a community of people who have problematic relationships with alcohol. There is no better support for self-destructive behaviours than peer support, especially for those behaviours about which people ordinarily feel unable to speak openly due to stigma and shame. The advice of a GP or an information leaflet about the health harms of alcohol should not be ignored, but the understanding of like-minded people has far greater power to alter the way we act as individuals. Furthermore, there are many reasons why a person won't confess their drinking habits to their GP or other health professional, ranging from fears over the involvement of Social Services and how this may threaten their family unit to worries about 'alcohol dependency' being added to medical records which may be picked up by an employer.

Aside from these concerns, it is often just uncomfortable and unpleasant to sit before another person and admit, 'I have a real problem with booze', not least because of the cultural normalisation of drinking in the West. We're often fearful that our inability to drink 'normally' could be viewed as a sign of weakness. Hence the common scenario of the heavy drinker stating his or her consumption as being around the fourteen unit mark, when in reality it's closer to one hundred-plus.

Online peer support such as Soberistas avoids all of these issues completely by allowing members to remain fully anonymous. In this way, Soberistas serves as a type of confessional service – a place where those who post can reveal long-held secrets to people who will almost definitely have been there and done it before them. This mutual sharing of innermost thoughts and worries combines to build a palpable sense of community, and Soberistas is, for me, the best example of a community I have ever happened upon.

Community, defined by Oxford Dictionaries as 'the condition of sharing or having certain attitudes and interests in common', is essential for human beings to feel understood and valid. In the modern world, traditional community life has largely been lost to a capitalist and secular society, with people living atomised existences, working long hours and relying increasingly on social media to connect with one another. Chatting to a neighbour over the garden fence is, for many people, a mere childhood memory. We often expend more energy expressing sympathy for the victims of a natural disaster occurring on the other side of the planet than for the infirm elderly person living on the same street as us who can no longer make it to the shops for food. This breakdown of the wider community has had an impact on our individual emotional states of wellbeing, for we *need* to feel as though we belong – it is a basic requirement of human beings.

A second substantial benefit of utilising an online peer support service such as Soberistas is that it helps with accountability. Promising yourself that you will not drink again after a major binge is, for many, insufficient for creating long-term motivation. It's all too easy to allow that sneaky inner voice to creep in the next day with its persuasive, soothing tones, ameliorating all of the nastiness and telling you that you don't *really* have a problem with booze. You're overreacting. But somehow, when you've written a blog (albeit anonymously) stating that yes, you finally acknowledge that you have an alcohol dependency and you want to stop permanently, it's not so easy to back out. When other people who truly understand your pain have offered you their wisdom and advice, it becomes quite difficult to disregard all of that and get stuck back into the booze again as soon as your hangover has dissipated.

One of the most popular pages of the Soberistas website is 'Personal Stories', a place where people post accounts of their drinking histories. It is with a massive sense of relief that many new members read these stories and realise that they are not alone, freakish or in some way bad purely because they cannot drink alcohol in moderate amounts. What an incredibly important step on the road to wellness it is to appreciate that alcohol dependency is, in fact, a widespread problem. It's affecting people from all walks of life – everyday people, well educated, kind and interesting people, who cannot stop drinking when they begin. It is not, as lots of us are prone to imagine when we're hiding our difficulties with alcohol from the world, something peculiar to the odd few. It is a hugely common issue that does not equate to the sufferer being unworthy on any level. This is a third reason why Soberistas can help – other people's experiences, as recorded on the site, resonate with new members, and that feeling of not being the only one is a brilliant starting point for becoming alcohol-free.

When everything looks bleak and you can't *ever* imagine living a life that does not prominently feature alcohol, it is incredibly helpful to witness the journeys of people who've already managed to kick the booze. There are lots of ex-drinkers on Soberistas who continue to visit the site regularly in order to share their insight and advice with newcomers. You can derive hope from real life examples of whatever it is you are trying to achieve. When you read about a person who once endured the most terrible existence because of their alcohol dependency but has since quit and is now happy and healthy, it's impossible not to take joy from that. Surely, you start to think, if she can do it then so can I. This person sounds as though they were once exactly like me – look at him now. Right there, before your eyes, is a mass of blindingly stark evidence that an alcohol-free life works very well indeed for people lacking an off-switch.

Between them, members of Soberistas who have successfully tackled their drinking problems possess a wealth of ideas and tips for becoming alcohol-free. These people know exactly what does and does not work on the path to quitting drinking, and they share their advice freely for all members to benefit from. I will always listen to a person with first-hand experience of *anything* before someone who has gleaned their information from a book. And especially in the case of alcohol dependency issues, the emotions and fears associated with this problem are such that I doubt people without personal knowledge could truly understand what works in terms of resolving things.

A key characteristic of Soberistas lies in its positivity. If I had not managed to find the plus points in quitting drinking, I suspect I would never have stuck to my sobriety, and I expressly wanted this to become the cornerstone of my new website's ethos. Firstly, let's examine the name – Soberistas. It denotes a way of life that is aspirational. Right at the beginning of a person's alcohol-free journey, it is perceived as the place they want to reach rather than being where they are right now (pissed off, hungover and miserable). Nobody wants to be known solely as an alcoholic, but you know what? Being labelled a Soberista is not bad at all.

To me, a Soberista equates to a strong, empowered and healthy individual who simply has the desire to carve out a brighter future for her or himself – a future that does not include alcohol. A Soberista is not defined by their past, but is someone focusing on the here and now who has the hope and determination to live a better life than the one they have been living. Yes, it's necessary to spend some time working on the issues behind our heavy drinking, and it's essential to practise self-analysis in an effort to understand ourselves more – this way we can avoid repeating old mistakes. But equally as important is concentrating on the present, existing in the moment and reminding ourselves just how far we have come in the fight against alcohol dependency. In employing the tag of 'Soberista', we can continually bolster our positive intentions as opposed to remaining mired in the miserable gloom of our dark drinking days.

I believe the trick to becoming and staying sober is to declutter and generally spring clean our lives, carrying out lots of internal work on all the issues that led to us drinking too much in the first place and visualising a new, improved version of ourselves to which we can aspire. Soberistas is full of examples and information on how to do all of this, and it's anchored firmly in Camp Positive. It absolutely is possible to iron out the wrinkles in our individual worlds, seek out more effective coping strategies and change all the bits of our lives that meant we were tempted to drink. It's a case of having sufficient faith in the fact that changes can and will materialise, and spending time on Soberistas helps this come to fruition.

A major trigger for many people in the initial phase of sobriety is boredom. Sitting about twiddling their thumbs can easily lead to a split-second decision to head out to the shops and make an impromptu alcoholic purchase. The chat room on Soberistas is a wonderful means of obtaining instant help in *not* caving into such temptations – when a person logs on and admits to having an urge to drink, a member of the site will invite the support, wisdom and friendship of the community which more often than not results in that trip to the shops never taking place. And because there are members located all over the world, there is always someone online at any given moment – something which is unique to internet-based peer support.

And finally, while there are advantages to be found in real life peer support groups, there are lots of people for whom reaching such help is impossible. Single parents, those with certain physical impairments or people living in remote areas do not have the option of attending meetings. For these people, an online resource is the *only* method at their fingertips (literally) to join a community of like-minded individuals either aiming to stop or who've already succeeded in stopping consuming alcohol.

I came up with the notion of a website aimed at people who have problematic relationships with alcohol because I felt alone. It seemed as though everyone I knew could handle their drink except me; none of them appeared to be possessed by the same demons as I was when it came to booze. I didn't conceive of these people plotting and calculating, desperately attempting to control their alcohol consumption in the same ways that I did – my friends all seemed to have a drink when they fancied one and never suffered terribly negative fallouts as a result. And so I was driven to build a community of people who felt the way I did about alcohol.

After almost four years of life, Soberistas has blossomed into not just a place to talk to like-minded friends about booze, as first intended, but an effective resource for quitting drinking. For all the reasons listed in this chapter, the website continues to succeed in positively influencing behaviour, ultimately leading to permanent changes in longstanding habits.

I must admit to loving Soberistas very much. It is an integral part of me, and I know it will always remain so.

T

Truth: The Inevitability Of Existence

As a drinker, I never allotted a great deal of thought to death. OK, that's not actually true; I did frequently wake up in the middle of the night with a dry mouth and the hangover from hell, beset by terrifying panic attacks over how I'd probably given myself cancer by smoking and drinking with such gusto throughout my entire adulthood. Those early-hours-of-the-morning anxieties, however, did not particularly lead me to any deep considerations of human mortality, nor did they throw up any existentialist epiphanies. They merely rendered me petrified, a scared little girl trapped by her incessant self-destructive behaviours.

As a sober person, I appreciate that there are no shields from the inevitability of death. Each and every one of us is inflicted and governed by the arrow of time. And my theory, as a totally non-scientific layperson, is that alcohol and the ingestion of other mind-altering drugs have been attractive to the human race for thousands of years precisely because they allow for a momentary escape from this devastating truth.

Animals have no concept of past and future, of

limited time, nor are they beset by the fear that existence might just be a pointless phenomenon. They just *are*, mindful in the extreme and blissfully untroubled by the reality of their own impending death. Just spend a few hours in the company of a dog and you'll understand what I mean.

Anthropologists from the University of Valladolid in Spain have compiled evidence supporting the fact that human beings were ingesting psychoactive drugs around 10,600 years ago. Fermenting jugs dating back to Neolithic times indicate that alcohol too has been a fixture in human life for millennia. Despite the common thinking regarding this early use of mind-altering substances as being purely for spiritual and ritualistic purposes, people have been drinking for thousands of years for other reasons.

As a species we crave an escape from the mundane by seeking out altered states of consciousness. There are, of course, several ways of achieving this: music, meditation, the arts and exercise to name but a few. But alcohol is by far the most normalised and acceptable means of elevating ourselves above the flat plains of predictability and on to a sojourn in an exciting parallel universe. It helps us to forget the boring and repetitive nature of daily life – the ironing, shopping, jobs we dislike and relationships that have grown past their sell-by date. It injects a sense of the unknown and takes us into a world tinged with the faint whiff of danger. Just before a big night out I would often suffer from an attack of butterflies, unsure as to where I would end up, with whom and doing what. That kind of wild unpredictability is difficult, if not impossible, to obtain without taking mind-altering substances.

In addition to this, drinking regularly shrinks our vantage point on life. As drinkers, we often begin to look forward only to the next weekend, the next Saturday night, the next big social event, as these are the major markers that divide our routine continuance. And when we adopt such a short-term view, the big and looming truth, the one that nobody wants to embrace, recedes into the distance. Its visibility is reduced; that unquestionable and deeply unsettling knowledge of our own inevitable death becomes harder to pin down. It hides behind a smokescreen of immediacy, instant pleasures and wanton escapism. But when we remove alcohol and subsequently this short-term perspective, we are left with endless plateaus of indistinguishability.

There is another means of cushioning the remorseless blow of mortality, which is religion. For those who believe in a God, the notion of slipping quietly from this life into the next remains a comfort to hang on to. We are told that Heaven is a beautiful and peaceful place, and even though it's not often spoken of overtly in these secular times, for those with faith it is an ever-present fender to oblivion.

And so what about the non-drinkers who are also non-believers? Personally I think we have to dig a bit deeper to locate a meaning of life. We have to search out new and different ways to depart the daily grind temporarily. It's no use pretending, hoping, that the innate desire to escape the humdrum briefly will simply disappear. It's been a feature of the human experience since the beginning of our time on Earth.

Since I stopped drinking, I have found peace in the acceptance of my own mortality. I've thought about dying a lot, considering what the point is of me being here at all. I acknowledge that much of the stuff I attach importance to on a daily basis is really quite meaningless – the rush to make an appointment on time or the panic over burning a slice of toast. And in weighing up these inconsequential fragments of day-to-day living I have come to the conclusion that, in the grand scheme of things, nothing is more significant than anything else. Ultimately, we will all become dust, together with the world around us.

Following this logic, it would be easy to reduce our lives to nothingness. There would be no purpose in getting out of bed, or finding a job, or going for a walk. From where would the motivating forces come that make us strive harder to achieve more? Why would we care about making friends or learning to drive a car? Why would anyone ever make the effort to learn to swim, buy beautiful furniture or have a haircut?

The reason behind people doing any of these things is that we are all actively seeking happiness and pleasure – we want to enjoy our lives to the maximum capacity, regardless of whether there will be anything left at all at the end. Hopeless optimists and relentless dreamers, many of us will pursue our dreams right up until the stage when we no longer can. It's essential to attach meaning to our lives to ensure that we get the most out of our limited time on the planet. For what is the point of living if each day is merely a desperate struggle to make it to the next?

But what *is* the meaning of life? The Dalai Lama said, 'If you want others to be happy, practise compassion. If you want to be happy, practise compassion.' This is the crux of the matter, and something I have only properly understood to be true since quitting drinking. With the omission of that short-term and narcissistic goal (i.e. escaping reality via the excessive consumption of alcohol) it becomes possible to extend our thinking and concerns to others over and above our own needs. In my old life, nothing could come between a truckload of booze and me – not even my closest family. If I wanted to drink, I was damn well going to drink. And the repercussions this had on those around me were not insignificant. I failed to pick up on subtleties and social nuances. I didn't consider whether the people I was with might actually wish to go home as opposed to staying in a bar for yet another round. I was self-absorbed and thick-skinned, too affected by the alcohol in my system to pick up on the many indicators that other people did not always share my outward enthusiasm for drunkenness.

But when you remove the drinking, you find compassion. And when you exercise compassion – both towards yourself and the people you meet and mix with throughout your life – you discover happiness. And this most simple of equations amounts to the key for a meaningful existence. It creates a purpose to life.

As soon as life takes on *real* meaning beyond an addiction-fuelled single point of focus, death in all of its frightening darkness can be transformed into something entirely new. Dying was once a terrifying concept to me because I didn't understand what *life* was about, and without a true reason to live, I didn't feel ready to face death. However, through recognising that the meaning of life is happiness, and to achieve this we must practise compassion for all human beings, including ourselves (and it's very important to remember that part), I have managed to steer myself away from dreading my own mortality and towards an acceptance of my humble place within the wider universe.

Many people fall into the trap of looking beyond themselves in order to achieve inner contentment – if only they could afford that new pair of shoes, or move house or get married, then they'd realise the happiness they have always been lacking. Drinking alcohol regularly feeds into this escapist mentality because we grow accustomed to avoiding dealing with daily challenges and uncomfortable emotions, utilising booze as an easy means of numbing away problems. Shopping addictions, gambling and overeating are other manifestations of the same entrenched issues – seeking a removal of ourselves from an uncomfortable reality and looking for happiness externally.

When these distractions are avoided and we focus instead on our emotions and face up to the truth of a situation, it becomes possible to draw on internal strength to move on. This builds self-reliance and confidence, and when this particular battle has been won, we experience feelings of pride and elation.

When we repeat this scenario often, without alcohol interfering in the natural order of things, it becomes increasingly clear that fulfilment and satisfaction in life are, in fact, derived from within. And with such self-confidence, we have the ability to demonstrate compassion towards others (as well as exercising self-compassion). At this point, the route to fulfilment, life and the meaning of it, our purpose on the planet and how to maintain a state of deep contentedness should be obvious.

And with this revelation comes an understanding of life as a big picture in all of its wonder – from birth right up until death. We are each of us no different from other animals: we are born, we exist and we die. Without alcohol in my life I could see this simplicity clearly, and simultaneously I ceased to fear my own mortality.

One of the hardest parts for me of adjusting to an alcohol-free life was to stop fearing the future. I was scared of not living enough, of being boring now that I was sober, of missing out and not fully enjoying myself. And I understood fairly quickly that I no longer had such a direct means of escaping my reality at my fingertips. There were instances when I felt frozen with fear at the thought that my life would now always be predictable and steady with no more dramas and crazy U-turns. I would perpetually have a clear idea about where I was heading.

Surprisingly, all of this didn't take an eternity to adjust to. And now I happily accept that life is something of a fluke. I don't take it for granted. I realise what a gift it is. The lengthening of my perspective – seeing much further into my distance than I ever did when the next boozy session was as far as I allowed my thoughts to wander – has brought me appreciation of and compliance with the natural order. I know what's heading my way. I have found a reason to live. And I now see that my path was always marked out as an alcohol-free one.

U

Uncritical of Other People's Drinking

In the early days of sobriety, it's entirely normal to feel bouts of extreme jealousy and resentment towards people who are still 'allowed to drink'. I did not enjoy one iota being around those who were knocking back the bevvies like nobody's business as I shuffled about awkwardly, feeling conspicuous with mineral water in hand. In fact, I don't think there has ever been a time in my life when I've harboured such negativity towards complete strangers as when I initially became alcohol-free.

I was seriously depressed about the fact that I could no longer drink (or at least not with any cast-iron guarantee for my health and safety). And because of how alcocentric western society is, I found it immeasurably hard being exposed to alcohol consumption wherever I found myself. Haircut? Here, have a glass of Prosecco. Early evening meal in a family-friendly restaurant with the kids? Here's a bottle of Pinot Grigio. Even the gym that I currently visit which runs hardcore boot-camp style classes has recently got in on the act, offering a glass of fizz to all newcomers. Imagine that – an hour of intense exercise washed down with a glass of booze.

Anyway, I digress.

The point is that when you finally reach the decision to stop drinking, even when you know it's for the best, other people's booze habits will impinge on your alcohol-free intentions. It's the world we live in, and it will feel odd in the first instance to have shifted from one side of the tracks to the other. But to help smooth the path to confident alcohol-free living, it's crucial to remember that other people's drinking has nothing to do with *your* relationship with booze. The sooner you wrap your head around this, the less chance there will be of you losing your way on the path to happy sobriety.

When you allow other people's drinking to creep into your consciousness, it can spark off the voice of a little drinking devil, whispering in your ear, 'So what if your sleep has improved, you've shed weight and saved money? You need to inject a little fun into your world – go on, get out and have a few drinks. What harm will it do?' And after a few weeks of feeling reasonably sure that you've cracked this alcohol-free malarkey, you could easily consider sliding back into your old shoes and throwing caution to the wind once again. If you have never fully let go of the latent urge to get pissed, it will be lurking just below the surface, waiting for the first excuse to encourage you to fall off the wagon. If other people's drinking has continually bothered you – either because you secretly wish to join them or because you've developed feelings of disdain towards anyone who dares to allow alcohol to pass their lips – then you have not reached a completely safe place.

Time helps with feeling OK about other people's drinking habits. Letting go of alcohol does resemble, in many ways, the bereavement process – the four stages of grief are commonly regarded as denial, depression, anger and acceptance, and it's typical to experience these emotional states in the aftermath of an alcohol dependency.

Alcohol constitutes the greatest love of many big drinkers' lives – I know it did for me. As I sank into the hellhole that was my divorce, sat among the tears and tissues arising out of a variety of deep disappointments and searched for a means of dragging myself from countless states of boredom and frustration, booze was always there for me. There was a delight in utilising something that altered my mood, made me not care so much about anything and never asked for a single thing in return…

Actually, that last point is not true at all. Booze demands *so* much from drinkers, and ultimately will take everything we've got in exchange for nothing. I couldn't grasp this at all when I was drinking – this crutch that we, as people dependent upon alcohol, grow to count on so desperately is an inordinately difficult thing to let go of. The void that we envisage opening up in its absence can appear too vast to fill with anything else. What could possibly replace that bottle of wine, which is only ever a shopping visit away and will reliably annihilate our negative feelings in one fell swoop?

Initially, denial will prevent most people from beginning to tackle their problematic relationship with booze. There will *always* be someone else to whom we can point, highlighting his or her alcohol issues as being far worse than our own. We don't drink in the morning; we don't touch vodka; we live in a nice house – right? And even if we possess the knowledge that all is not well, it can take years – decades even – before we've worked through the denial phase and can finally acknowledge that we really should stop drinking for good.

The second stage of the grieving process, depression, is about the flat lining – the realisation that this is it, permanent sobriety. Never again will I get shitfaced. For the rest of my days I'm going to be straight. This is a hard concept to wrap our heads around, and now's probably the period when other people's drinking will be the most challenging to cope with. There is a No Man's Land in between alcohol dependency and happy, comfortable sobriety where you *know* that you want to stop the madness but are yet to appreciate the true benefits of being alcohol-free. It strikes you as unfair, completely and utterly unfair, that everyone else (as you will no doubt perceive it) can still enjoy a drink while you must deny yourself this basic pleasure in life. You will question the whys and ruminate over the perceived upsides of consuming alcohol – once the rose-tinted glasses are in place and the sheer awfulness of it all has dissipated.

During the depression phase, it's likely that you will experience feelings of loneliness and deep insecurity (see the chapter 'Soberistas' for help to get through this stage). It can be very difficult to cope with such a wide and varied range of emotions as regret, guilt, not being understood by the world at large, boredom and sadness, and all without the crutch that you've relied upon, possibly for decades, whenever you've felt down or stressed – alcohol.

It may appear that life has little meaning without alcohol and you'll never find a way of being happy again without it featuring regularly in your daily routine. And as the days dawdle by and the horizon stretches ever further into the distance, other people's drinking will be suddenly magnified. This is an important element of the adjustment from being a heavy drinker to being sober. I think it's necessary to observe the ways others consume alcohol to draw distinctions between them and you – what happens when certain individuals drink and how is it different from the way alcohol impacts on you? As I asked myself these questions, I became aware of a very real truth: the things I'd done when drunk, and the ways in which I'd often behaved as a result of being dependent upon alcohol, were not things I recognised in most other people.

I saw, for example, an obsession in myself with regard to alcohol. It topped pretty much everything else in terms of how I spent my spare time. I was skilled in incorporating booze into everyday situations, even the occasions when there was really no need for drinking alcohol whatsoever (children's birthday parties, a trip to the zoo, visiting the cinema). I rarely embarked on the journey home after an evening in the pub without commandeering someone into accompanying me – along with several bottles of wine from the late night supermarket. And when I quit drinking, the people I knew quit doing these things. A lot of the time, it had been upon my persuasion that drinking sessions had either continued past their shelf life or had begun in the first place. Other people did not drink in the same way that I did.

As the penny dropped, I inched ever closer to the next bereavement stage: anger. I was downright pissed off that I apparently had this affliction while other people, who also liked to drink, did not. This bothered me for a very long time. I would see other people downing cold alcoholic drinks in pub gardens, or watch jovial groups of friends falling out of bars, laughing and partying into the night, and I would angrily ask myself, 'Why me?' I was cross with the alcohol industry and annoyed with the government for not putting into place more stringent restrictions on the sale of alcohol. Whenever I noticed an advert for booze I was filled with rage, indignant that this addictive drug was being peddled to unknowing individuals all over the world.

A lot of this anger was actually a positive thing for me, because it spurred me on to do something about the global alcohol problem. Ultimately, I doubt I would have created Soberistas had it not been for this time in my life. But negative anger is not sustainable, and it doesn't lead to a calm and content life.

Stage four of the grieving process, acceptance,

turned out to be a distant and hard-won attainment for me. I suspect it took around three years for me to take on board that, psychologically and physiologically, I'm not wired the same as people who have the ability to moderate their alcohol consumption. It wasn't merely a case of accepting this fact but of being in a position where I could honestly say that I am *happy* not to drink alcohol. I wouldn't want to drink it, even if I could control my intake.

How did this transformation occur? Time was the main factor, just as it is when we are recovering emotionally from the death of a loved one. In order to work through all the emotions associated with quitting drinking, time is an essential.

The most noticeable thing about reaching the final phase of the grieving process was that I no longer felt jealous or bitter with regard to other people's drinking. I still feel strongly that the alcohol industry is given far too much freedom in marketing and advertising their products, and I believe the government's actions on the alcohol-related public health crisis in the UK fall far short of being satisfactory, but I'm not angry any more.

Alcohol should not define a person. When you make the choice to quit drinking and subsequently undergo the turbulent and life-changing journey of learning to live without alcohol, it makes no sense to let it continue to control your emotions. Other people will never stop drinking because they have been told to or because they've been at the receiving end of a disapproving frown and a wagging finger. In fact, experience would suggest the opposite is true – tell anyone with an emotional or physical dependency on an addictive substance or behaviour to stop and they'll go and do it more. There is only one person who will ever provide the impetus to quit drinking and that is the drinker her or himself.

One of the most enjoyable consequences of letting go of my alcohol dependency has been the effect it has had on my mental health. I am calm, and immeasurably more tolerant of other people's opinions and differences. Employing the good sense and wisdom of Buddhist philosophy, I believe we all need to follow our own individual path in life. I established Soberistas for people who knew they wanted to stop drinking – for the ones who had already arrived at that crossroads in life where they recognised that alcohol no longer did anything positive for them. It was never intended to be a temperance movement, a means of converting the masses.

I have discovered, surprisingly, that simply as a result of my own approach to alcohol – the fact that I have opted to live the rest of my days with clarity and a healthy, respectful attitude towards my mind and body – that many of my friends and family have followed suit. Not complete sobriety for most, but a far more cautious relationship with alcohol and a realisation that it's entirely possible to have a fulfilling and rewarding time without booze featuring so prominently on the agenda.

When bitterness and anger rule our minds, when we find it really tough being in the company of anyone who is drinking, it stands to reason that we are not yet content in terms of our own relationships with alcohol and sobriety. Time allows for a mellowing of this negativity. For me, it was a sign that I was completely over my drinking issues when I could sit comfortably in the presence of someone who was consuming alcohol. This does not mean I'm untroubled by the destruction that excessive alcohol consumption wields upon society, and it definitely does not amount to apathy with regard to helping people who want to stop drinking, but it does mean that I am sufficiently secure within my own sobriety not to attempt to enforce my beliefs on others who perhaps have not endured the same difficulties through alcohol as me.

Whenever we are overly concerned with anyone else's behaviour (whether it be their drinking or anything else), it can be an indicator that we're deflecting attention away from our own actions. And in the case of the journey to being happily alcohol-free, I strongly feel that we'd be far better off focusing on our own relationship with alcohol than that of the people around us. If we lead by positive example, the chance of our loved ones being influenced by our non-drinking status is significant.

Remember the four stages of grieving: denial, depression, anger and acceptance, and try to remain mindful of where you are along the process. Time heals all, including the negativity you might feel towards other people who are drinking alcohol.

V

Vanity: Nothing Wrong With Loving How You Look Now You Aren't a Booze Hound

An app was launched a few years ago which cleverly illustrates a person's face ten years down the line, should that individual continue to drink alcohol heavily. The concept is simple: take a photo of yourself then enter in the amount of booze you consume over the course of an average week, and hey presto! Your face will appear, all blotchy, bloated and red, with sunken eyes and dull, dehydrated skin. The app came out not long after I quit drinking, and although I wasn't in a place where I needed reminding why I wanted to be alcohol-free, the innovation struck me as being a cute means of altering behaviour.

On the flip side, from the moment we enter this world, we are subjected to a constant stream of positive, glamorous imagery suggesting that alcohol is not only innocuous in terms of health harms but a necessary ingredient for anyone wishing to vamp up his or her sex appeal. An old Bacardi advert sticks in my mind with its depiction of a Latina woman, all long, dark hair and sultry good looks, dancing in a hot, sweaty club surrounded by admiring male onlookers. Obviously all those featured in the advert were resplendent with glasses of Bacardi, the liquid swilling around in tumblers topped up with lime and ice – refreshing, sophisticated, sexy, charged with energy.

The following is an extract from the Advertising Standards Authority website, the ASA being the UK's independent regulator for advertising across all media:

> *The stringent rules, which apply across all media and are mandatory, place a particular emphasis on protecting young people; alcohol ads must not be directed at people under 18 or contain anything that is likely to appeal to them by reflecting youth culture or by linking alcohol with irresponsible behaviour, social success or sexual attractiveness.*

I do find it remarkable that the majority of alcohol commercials find their way past these guidelines, particularly when one considers the UK's alcohol advertising standards are among the strictest in the world. Alcohol marketing is so inextricably bound up with sex and sexual freedom that it is almost laughable that the ASA purports to ban adverts containing anything linking booze to sexual attractiveness. Even adverts which, ostensibly, are intended to be humorous (I'm thinking of the

Foster's lager brand, focusing on Australia's beach culture) feature good-looking women in tiny bikinis and men bearing a number of characteristics (general laddish behaviour, football obsession, 'lightweight' sexism) that are highly sought-after by the target audience.

Daniel Craig, star of the latest James Bond films, brought all the glamour of the longstanding spy movies to the world of alcohol advertising when he appeared in a Heineken / *Spectre* promotional campaign in 2015. In an article about the Daniel Craig commercial, Mark Sweney for the *Guardian* newspaper (21 September 2015) quotes Hans Erik Tuijt, director of global sponsorship at Heineken:

> *There is always a lot of criticism* [about Bond]. *Why not a woman? We thought it was an excellent time to introduce a woman of the world. If you look at other campaigns, it is always a man of the world that saves the day* [alongside Bond]. *We thought it was time to introduce a woman of the world* [to the campaign]. *It is the first time the Heineken character is a woman.*

All well and good, and a clever means of highlighting Heineken as a forward-thinking brand that favours gender equality – except that the 'woman of the world' in the advert fits the western female stereotype of sexual attractiveness and wears a bikini throughout. Furthermore, when hasn't James

Bond been regarded as sexy, dashing and something of a womaniser? This is his unique selling point, or USP. James Bond equals sex, and Heineken has been rather clever in riding the publicity wave of the film.

The *Spectre*/Heineken partnership and the aforementioned Bacardi adverts constitute just two examples of how alcohol is frequently portrayed in the UK, despite the ASA's supposed strict regulations on the matter. The conclusion of such unfettered marketing is, for most adults, an unwavering link between booze and sex, glamour and sophistication.

And yet, we know the opposite to be true. When I quit drinking at the age of thirty-five, I suspect I escaped by the narrowest of margins any permanent physical damage as a result of my alcohol intake. After undergoing a FibroScan a couple of years into my sobriety, I was reassured to discover that my liver was 'very healthy' (in the words of the hepatologist who delivered the results). But for many people, the effect alcohol has upon their exterior physicality can provide a greater degree of motivation for ditching the booze than the havoc it is causing on the inside. Hence the invention of the app mentioned at the start of this chapter.

Most people possess a basic desire to look presentable, and the manner in which alcohol is marketed routinely leads to us thinking that, by drinking, we are boosting our attractiveness. However, alcohol consumption on a regular basis does nothing positive for our appearance whatsoever, and the depiction of beautiful people drinking gallons of booze in films and elsewhere in popular culture is nothing but a complete myth. Let's consider the facts.

The following is an abridged extract from an article first posted on Soberistas.com entitled 'Facing Facts' and written by me, Lucy Rocca:

Alcohol is a toxin and, like any other poison we might ingest, our bodies will go into overdrive in an effort to be rid of it. The skin is the largest organ in the body and is very important for excretion, i.e. getting rid of waste (along with the kidneys, bowel and lungs – we 'breathe out' all sorts of waste, including alcohol). Consequently the skin becomes overworked if it continually has to excrete alcohol (you can often smell that morning-after-alcohol smell on people), which is partly why it can look exhausted when people are drinking heavily.

A noticeable effect of drinking too much alcohol is that the face can become flushed and red. This occurs because alcohol dilates the blood vessels directly beneath the skin. Over time, the capillaries surrounding the nose can burst causing a permanent redness – this can affect not only the nose but also the entire facial area. Another unhealthy outcome for our skin when we drink too much is dehydration. Alcohol is a diuretic substance, and thus, when consumed in excess, it causes dryness to the skin, which can feel scaly to the touch and also be prone to fine lines and premature ageing. This is worsened by smoking (and it is often the case that people smoke more when drinking alcohol) as both these habits deplete the body of Vitamin A, crucial for protection against free radicals.

Bloating is another frequent complaint associated with drinking too much alcohol on a regular basis – again, this is linked to the fact that alcohol is dehydrating. The body retains what water it has in order to combat the diuretic nature of alcohol. Consequently, cheeks can look puffy and under-eye bags are often accentuated. In addition, alcohol prevents good quality sleep and the resulting tiredness can exacerbate bloating in the face.

Due to the toxicity of alcohol, it has a highly detrimental effect on the liver, the organ tasked with ridding the body of any poisons (alcohol being a major example within the western world). When the liver is placed under strain, it is less effective at synchronising all the complex pathways that are responsible for keeping the body running efficiently, and so the whole system gets silted up. The end result is often an unhealthy looking complexion characterised by blotchiness, dullness and blemishes.

As well as the above less than encouraging summary of alcohol and its effects on the skin, drinking too much usually worsens conditions such as psoriasis and rosacea.

The sum total of this wide-ranging damage inflicted upon our bodies as a result of excessive alcohol consumption is not something we would recognise in the faces and bodies of the people featured in alcohol adverts. There is a basic lie in operation in this respect, although once we become aware of this lie then it's far easier to ignore.

On a brighter note, being alcohol-free really does have numerous positive effects upon our physical states. When we're not pouring bottles of toxic liquid down our throats on a frequent basis, the body is able to recover from all the years of boozing that have gone before.

Not only does adopting an alcohol-free lifestyle (in most circumstances) allow for the body to repair itself internally – even after years of heavy drinking – it also kick starts a cycle of positivity in terms of how we look on the outside. When we're suffering from a debilitating hangover and feeling wretched from head to toe, there's no amount of make-up or face cream that will fix things. In my latter drinking years I was guilty of trowelling on the foundation in many a desperate attempt to make myself look presentable, although I may as well not have bothered. My eyes were always dull, never sparkling, and my skin was waxy, with big open pores being a dead giveaway as to my secret boozing sessions. There is an expression that springs to mind at this juncture: 'You can't gild a lily'.

Beauty emerges from the inside. When a person is healthy because they're eating well, sleeping properly, drinking sufficient water and not poisoning their body with alcohol, they exude attractiveness. Those images we see in alcohol advertisements of youthful, sexy people, holding an alcoholic drink as they laugh and flirt with the opposite sex, are as real as St. Elmo's fire, a phenomenon of luminous plasma created by a gap in electrical charge which held many sailors out at sea in awe due to its uncanny resemblance to fire. But it was merely an illusion. When we buy into the myth that drinking equates to sexiness, we are chasing a similar illusion – lusting after the unattainable.

As a drinker I would periodically embark on detoxes, although these never extended to my being sober or stopping smoking. I would cut out caffeine, up my water consumption and eat loads of fruit and vegetables, but there is no diet on the planet that can outmanoeuvre regular and heavy alcohol use. In addition to how alcohol affected my looks, I hated myself, and usually walked around with a nervous disposition and a fierce glare aimed at anyone who dared try to make eye contact with me. I carried the weight of the world on my shoulders, and the only time I ever appeared to be carefree and confident was after downing a couple of drinks – beyond that amount and my words would begin to slur and I'd stumble when walking (never especially attractive).

As our confidence increases and the trail of destructive behaviours arising out of drinking excessively begins to diminish, an internal transformation occurs that gradually starts to colour our external selves, too. There is a haunted look I occasionally notice in people, and I recognise it because I once used to have it. It's a product of bearing that big, guilty secret that we drink too much, often by ourselves. But when we become free of alcohol, that look disappears – we start to hold ourselves with an element of pride and dignity. We feel worthy as opposed to being plagued by the shameful weight of alcohol dependency. And this change in self-image has a real and noticeable effect on our appearance – it's palpable.

Throw in the fact that the pounds begin to drop off for lots of people who put an end to their boozy ways and that virtuous circle keeps on turning. After years of carting about more weight than you would like, it can be enormously motivational to find that, without the empty calories of alcohol, it all magically disappears. When you look in the mirror and notice the fact that you look better, it's a huge incentive for not going back to your erstwhile alcohol habit. And with less weight, it becomes easier and more appealing to start exercising – which in itself helps you to look and feel even better.

Drinking costs a lot of money, so when you quit you'll find that you have extra cash in the bank. It's a lovely feeling to treat yourself to new clothes, a beauty treatment or membership at a gym with money once thrown away on a toxic substance that brought mostly misery and self-loathing. And the beauty that arises from a healthy, non-drinking lifestyle is real, unlike the unattainable falsity of the images we are presented with by the alcohol industry – whose only motivation for creating such delusional ideals is profit.

In the UK there exists among some quarters a rather perverse belief that we shouldn't show off too much or fancy ourselves when we choose to dress smartly or take a little pride in our appearance. This attitude doesn't exist so noticeably in, say, Italian or French cities, where people enjoy putting effort into how they look to the outside world. I think we are all influenced to a degree by this insidious thinking and can tend to play down our physical attributes as a result.

Well, I would say in response to this approach, 'Stuff that!' We get one life, one chance. We should celebrate everything about ourselves that we like, especially after we have won the potentially long and challenging fight against the bottle and are finally able to approve of what we see in the mirror. Buy beautiful clothes with all that money not spent on booze, have your hair done, join a gym and start to feel great about yourself. As your inner confidence grows at the same rate as your outward appearance improves, you will feel human again. And not simply at a base level, but with pride and self-worth – things that alcohol robs you of. Everyone in your life will love watching you emerge from the ruin you once were as a drinker. Embrace it, admire yourself and love the person you are, free from booze.

When you drink too much for too long, you can wind up accepting a very low standard of *everything* in life, and it takes time to realise that good things *can* (and often do) become the norm. If there is one advert that you should take note of – and I mean for the message rather than for the products being sold – it's the one with the slogan: 'Because you're worth it'. Because you are. We all are.

W

Wine Witch Wisdom
(and Other Handy Tips I've Picked
Up Along the Way)

I stopped drinking in a totally unprepared and cold turkey fashion. I didn't ready myself by studying loads of books, I didn't have a support system like Soberistas to turn to during my darkest hours (of which there were many), and I had no clue that lots of people use certain tactics to help them get through the initial, most challenging period of sobriety. But over the years I've picked up a few tips and ideas that are widely utilised by those aiming to live an alcohol-free life, and in this chapter I'll share them with you.

Wine Witch

Different people will adopt a variety of names for the voice that tells you, very convincingly, to pour yourself a drink amid your efforts to stay sober. Wolfie, Addict Head and Wine Witch are all alternatives for the personification of a booze craving. Whatever works. As far as I'm concerned, it's extremely helpful to identify the craving voice within and separate it from your rational mind. Once you can compartmentalise those nagging persuasions and understand that it is the addiction you're hearing, it becomes immeasurably easier to plough on through the urges and stick to the sober path.

Essentially, this is just mindfulness – an awareness of our thoughts and recognition that not every one that passes through the mind is true. We can be selective about the thoughts we pay attention to and discard the rest. Adopting a regular meditation practice really helps with developing an acute understanding of the mind, enabling the process of thought selection.

When we first stop drinking (or indeed begin to break any longstanding habit), it can be supremely simple to believe that each craving, every thought we have telling us to drink/eat/smoke, is derived from us: our real self. The thoughts appear entirely rational as they're usually backed up with a whole host of reasonable justifications for ditching the healthier lifestyle choices we have been striving to stick to. But in actual fact, these deliberations are merely an incarnation of old habits dying hard – they're the neurological pathways we have laid down over years and years of repetitive behaviours desperately fighting against being rewired.

The term Wine Witch helps as these persuasive taunts are then ascribed to another person, and therefore they are easier to ignore – especially if we mentally visualise the speaker of them as being evil and intent on spoiling our newfound happiness. I guess it's easier to fight against someone else rather than our own minds.

After not drinking for over five years and having read countless books on Buddhism and mindfulness, together with numerous insightful blogs and comments on Soberistas, I can't believe that when I first began my sober life I had absolutely no knowledge whatsoever of the Wine Witch. I would listen to those voices and cravings, finding it unbearably hard at times not to cave in to what they were saying and go out for a bottle of wine.

But equipped with this knowledge, you are standing yourself in good stead right at the beginning of your alcohol-free journey. Envisage that craving voice as a separate entity, ascribe it a name, and then enjoy telling it to f*** off whenever it attempts to swing your intentions back to booze.

Urge surfing

Here's a handy titbit of information that I wish I'd have known back in the early days. Sitting alongside the above Wine Witch strategy, this provides you with some ammo when the cravings strike. Generally speaking, cravings last for no longer than half an hour, and usually much less than this. Urge surfing refers to the concept of sitting out the craving – recognising it for what it is and appreciating that it will only last for a few minutes.

When you imagine that the uncomfortable sensation of craving an alcoholic drink is permanent, it can be virtually impossible to ignore. However, when you understand that it's temporary, it becomes eminently more manageable to sit with the feelings until they pass. A common reaction to any uncomfortable emotion is to judge it as negative and want rid of it, but if we can adopt a mindful approach to cravings this will rob them of much of their power.

When you sense a craving arising, sit down and take a few deep breaths. Centre yourself and focus on how you are feeling physically. Are you aware of any particularly unpleasant sensations in certain parts of the body (a knotted stomach, for example)? Keep on breathing, in through the nose and out through the mouth, and maintain your concentration on the physical manifestations of the craving.

Accept the effects that the craving is having upon you without judging them as bad or good. Set a stopwatch if you think you'll need to be reminded as to the expected length of the craving (you can set the stopwatch for however many minutes your cravings usually last for). All you need to promise yourself is that during this time you won't cave in and buy and/or drink alcohol.

An alternative method of urge surfing is to busy yourself with a task that you expect to take up around half an hour of your time – cleaning the oven, bagging up old clothes for the charity shop or washing the car. It doesn't matter what it is, but if it absorbs all of your attention for the designated time span of a craving, it will do the job just fine.

Find a delicious alcohol-free drink to fill the gap

When you're absolutely gagging for a beer or glass of wine, it will help enormously if you have available in the house a replacement drink that really hits the spot. Some people find alcohol-free beer to be ideal; others prefer a tasty cordial with sparkling mineral water and loads of ice. If you're up for putting in a bit more effort, there are countless gorgeous mocktail recipes available on the internet. The trick is to be prepared and have either the drink or the ingredients for it to hand: it could mean the difference between staying sober and not. Some of my favourites are the Bottle Green cordials (Pomegranate and Elderflower, for instance) and Erdinger Alcohol-Free Wheat Beer.

HALT

This acronym is another useful tool for beating the booze that I was totally unaware of until I began reading up on quitting drinking. It stands for Hungry, Angry, Lonely, Tired – the four conditions to avoid at all costs when in the early stages of sobriety. I would add another one to this list (although where it fits into the acronym I'm not sure) which is Boredom.

Alcohol contains such a substantial amount of sugar that after sustained and heavy consumption of it, our bodies can be left reeling – not only craving alcohol but also the sugar. Having ample supplies of healthy snacks close to hand can stave off hunger pangs as well as alcohol cravings (nuts, dried fruit, rye bread, hummus and porridge are all good here). This takes care of the first issue of the HALT reminder – don't let yourself grow too hungry!

Anger is a common emotion for triggering a desire to get wasted. Who, as a drinker, hasn't immediately reached for the bottle following an argument with a friend or partner, or hit the pub straight after work because their boss has done a magnificent job of pissing them off? Anger is a tough state of mind to sit with and it's normal to want to eradicate it as quickly as possible. However, we can employ methods of dealing with anger other than drinking it away. A brisk walk, run, or any other form of cardiovascular exercise is perfect for getting whatever's bothering you out of your system. Likewise, locking yourself in the bathroom and running a lovely, bubbly bath by candlelight can help to calm you down and restore a sense of perspective. Talking to a good friend and sounding off about your grievances can also help. Find a way to manage your anger that doesn't involve alcohol and be sure to turn to this new coping mechanism whenever rage begins to bubble up inside.

Loneliness can be another major reason for drinking too much. People may surround us all day yet leave us feeling incredibly lonely. Alcohol often seems appealing for its ability to diminish loneliness, although in the long term it frequently reduces our intercommunication skills and renders us even more isolated.

Feeling lonely when you're in a relationship or in contact with a good number of friends can happen because you are with the *wrong* sorts of people. Meeting new friends who are on the same wavelength restores a sense of connectedness and will really help in putting an end to feeling lonely. Joining a club opens the door to meeting new people, and perhaps assessing old relationships for their true value might be worth considering. And if it's just a case of not seeing the people you *do* like enough, be sure to pick up the phone and ring someone for a chat or arrange a coffee together. Human contact has an immense power to alter our perspective completely, something I often find myself surprised by, so go ahead and utilise it.

The last word of the HALT acronym – tired – is of supreme importance. I don't know about you, but even when alcohol is removed from the equation, if I haven't had sufficient sleep then the world is a dark and terrible place. Our outlook is drastically altered when we're tired, with positivity being in short supply and a tendency arising to lose all faith in ourselves. In the initial period of living free from alcohol it's not uncommon to be overwhelmed with tiredness as the body repairs itself. Allow yourself the time to go with the desire to rest and get into the habit of creating a soothing bedtime routine. The basic needs of eating healthily and sleeping enough are of huge benefit in the early weeks of sobriety, so neglect either at your peril.

And finally, my own addition to HALT: boredom.

It takes a while to grow accustomed to being with yourself, liking who you are, so don't be worried about seeking out distractions whenever you find yourself with itchy feet. Join a club (I've said it before and I'll say it again: hobbies are good for you) or meet a friend, start running or sign up to yoga classes. Buy a box set and watch the whole damn thing in a week, just don't allow the dreaded boredom to creep in.

When you are new to learning about who you really are minus alcohol and you're walking on shaky sober ground, keep busy, be rested, don't go hungry and develop a knack of separating your addict voice from the rest of you. Follow these rules and you will make life much easier for yourself.

X

X-Factor (Finding that Thing that Fills the Booze Gap)

Other than 'M – Mindfulness', I suspect that 'X' will be the most important chapter of this book in terms of what's going to help you stay sober. It's also the chapter that I feel the most passionately about.

You won't have a clue what your X-factor is right at the start of your alcohol-free life. The only X-factor that will have been familiar to you as a drinker is alcohol, with its irritatingly all-consuming tentacles that wind up characterising your whole existence. When you first dabble in drinking, it's almost certainly without the knowledge that alcohol possesses the ability to sweep aside the many nuances – the beautiful, unique components that comprise you as an individual – and with a subtlety of immense proportions. You won't even recognise the process as it's happening. Slowly, the enthusiasm you once felt for all sorts of things, great and small, will be dismantled and neglected, lost completely to a perpetual urge to drink. Drink and be drunk, and nothing else shall get in the way.

But this thing that we are all searching for as human beings, and which so many people misguidedly believe is swimming around at the bottom of a bottle of booze, is the key to contentment. It's what fills us up emotionally and enables us to walk with grace and dignity through a life of our own perfect design. It is an intangible, impossible to define, but when we have it, we absolutely know it's there.

Throughout my drinking years I was seeking this sense of inner peace, and the closest I could get to it was when I allowed myself to slip into a parallel universe where my conscious mind became muddled with substances. Then I was able to transcend this world and momentarily inhabit a different place. And it didn't stop there. My old X-factor was born out of an entire lifestyle; it emerged from the relationships I had with people who also enjoyed hedonism. We refused to conform, and via the frequent escapism that heavy alcohol and drug use bring, we tried to establish ourselves as individuals. It was in the music we listened to and the dropping out of the system; the days spent lost to psychedelic bubbles and come-downs endured together in shared houses with curtains drawn and smoke-filled rooms.

Alcohol alone paved the way for me to obtain this sense of self once I'd decided I would no longer take illegal drugs. I had a baby and grew up, but that core 'me' didn't disappear with the arrival of a cot, nappies and responsibilities. She was still there, in and among it all, desperate for a voice, striving to find a platform. And during my twenties, I believed that alcohol delivered those things in a way that was entirely acceptable and above board.

What is it, then, this thing we are all searching for? It lies at the heart of all the adverts we see on the television, and in the magazine images we browse that taunt us with unobtainable ideals – the life we *should* be leading: one in which we are thinner, happier, fitter, more fulfilled, cooler, richer, braver, more popular. This magical recipe we are lusting after is not something that is easily acquired. We won't be able to find it (with any permanence) in booze or shopping or gambling, or anything else devoid of meaning. That stuff is merely there to distract us from the real life, the one that matters.

It happens, very naturally, when we reach a stage in life where we begin to understand the bigger picture.

I understand the X-factor as something that occurs when we begin to experience a connection with our personal histories. This in turn feeds into an appreciation of who we are as unique and wonderful human beings. When we are numbing our senses and emotions with alcohol or any other mind-altering drug, we are categorically unable to achieve this state of consciousness. We have no idea about who we are and what makes us tick. Our gut instincts are consistently muted, and the very things that we believe ourselves to be enjoying are most likely the constructions of our dependencies. We may imagine that we find fulfilment in an afternoon spent drinking with friends, but if we omitted the alcohol, would that same innate pleasure remain? Is it the addictive properties of alcohol that make this activity so appealing rather than the interactions with other people? We cannot answer this question until we are alcohol-free, because the power of addiction is such that it dramatically colours our personalities and thoughts.

So we remove the booze and start experiencing life in a natural, non-blinkered manner, and then what? Does this X-factor, this beautiful inner peace that everyone wants so badly, emerge like a rising sun? No, not really. It doesn't happen that way. This thing materialises when we hit the floor and regroup our inner self. It is born out of humility. It slowly comes to the fore when we lose our grip on the safety nets that we've clung to for so long and finally allow ourselves to go into free-fall.

Excessive alcohol use has a strange effect on the human spirit, frequently turning the drinker into a dichotomy of narcissism and self-loathing. On the one hand we despise ourselves for all the wrongs that alcohol has brought upon us, and on the other we can feel strangely untouchable and defiant, governed by a belief that the world revolves around us and everyone notices us and our self-imposed level of importance. This is, of course, an illusion. Without the booze, it blows away like an autumn leaf dancing along the pavement, and what is often left behind is an overwhelming notion that we are nothing after all. We are insignificant, and the very thing that made us glow brightly like stars in the night sky – alcohol – has been stolen from us. Without it, we are reduced to boring nobodies. Alcohol constituted the bullish interior that helped us stand out from mediocrity, and when it's gone, we become mere husks of all that went before.

This feeling of being adrift with no sense of purpose is something that many erstwhile heavy drinkers will undergo when they put down the bottle for good. Which is a good thing, because it's part of the process of recalibration. As a drinker, it's easy to coast along without ever drawing on the internal resolve that we are all equipped with to get through life. Alcohol numbs the struggles and so that fighting spirit sits untouched, never being granted its glory moment. But when we stop drinking and start to feel pain, and regret, and anger, and all the other normal emotional conditions that we *should* be feeling, we give ourselves the opportunity to be victors – we prove to ourselves that we can beat anything.

It's this process that starts the wheels in motion for pinpointing a sense of self – recognition of who we are as individuals. It's pride stemming from the fact that we have felt pain and stood up to it; we have battled through and emerged the other side complete with scars, blood, sweat and tears, and the knowledge that we can deal with life – any of it. When we arrive at this realisation, we stop being frightened of the world, and in that moment it's as though the shrouds that have always masked our reality fall away. We become privy at last to all the opportunities and wonders of the planet, and simultaneously we can see that we are equal to every other human being on it, which instantly distinguishes those self-made barriers to fulfilment.

Is it fear that prevents us from putting down the bottle? Are we so scared of the person we might become when we're let loose that we just keep on pouring in a desperate bid never to have to find out? We erect doors as drinkers – doors closed to establishing a relationship with ourselves. And when we open those doors, all the internal walls crumble. The ways in which we have allowed fear of nothing in particular to rule us with an iron fist disintegrate. What is left is a person free from shackles who is allowed to *live*.

Now, free from alcohol, you will be able to launch yourself on the world and immerse yourself in it, love it, breathe it all in and establish connections with things that will rock you, inside and out. These things will come in all sorts of shapes and sizes. For me, they are the heron I occasionally observe flying upstream in the woods, its enormous wings creating sound as they part the air; the smell of my dog's hot, sweaty body when I bend down to kiss her in the middle of a long run; the true mental contact I make with my daughters when none of us is curtailed by a secret self-consciousness or negative thought, and we laugh real belly laughs together; being immersed totally in listening to music I love which seeps into my soul and transports me to another world; lying on the grass, baking in the hot sun; standing at the peak of a mountain, staring at miles and miles of land devoid of noise pollution or any sign of human inhabitancy; fixating on the moon partly concealed by clouds and acknowledging it as a three-dimensional entity, not just a silver disc in the sky;

watching griffon vultures circling with intent high above the Andalusian hills; experiencing the true emotion of love and of being loved by another; waking up and feeling grateful and alive, and knowing that I am doing my best.

The discovery of the things that centre you and make you feel vital is a monumental one, for they are real and valid, bringing with them none of the destruction of alcohol. You can tap into a higher state of consciousness when you are sober. This is to be fully embraced. But it's of equal importance to let go of all the fallacies of superficiality, the belief that you will find contentment in the emptiness of consumerism.

My life was a shallow one when I drank. I was caught up in myself, my problems were magnified to the point of obscuring everything that mattered, and I was hell bent on finding the thing that would make it all OK. I looked for it in men, for the most part, utterly unable to dissect my relationships to see that they were no good. I lived for drinking, craved not being present in the world and therefore missed untold wonders. I had no real time for the inherent beauty of my environment – a walk in the countryside was just another excuse to have a pint; skiing in the French Alps with my best friend, who I should have treasured far more than I did, was an opportunity to get blasted in the mountain bar. While there, I failed to notice the sparkling white peaks, or at least I failed to notice that they were enough. A holiday in my mid-thirties, when I was young and vibrant, taken with a person I had a true connection with – spiritually and mentally – and set in a place of breath-taking natural allurement, and where was I? Lost on a mission to circumvent the whole lot.

Alternatively, I would be so engrossed in my active self-hatred and lack of meaningful association with the majority of the human race that I'd walk along with shoulders hunched and my face screaming out that I did not want contact with anyone. I was firing off poisoned darts as I walked, face bleak and uncommunicative, unwilling to close the gap that so clearly positioned me as alone. I would buy clothes then hate how I looked in them, despising the mirror. I'd have my hair restyled and then not leave the house because I was so supremely self-conscious. I was out of balance, off-kilter in every single aspect of my life. I had no clue as to what might bring me happiness, and would have been aghast at the thought of trying to find a deeper sense of meaning without alcohol. Alcohol, I imagined, was the only thing I could rely upon for a brief interlude from the drudgery.

As it turned out, it was alcohol that was preventing me from experiencing my X-factor. And it's the discovery of that special inner feeling that's allowed me to stay very happily sober for so many years. Since quitting the booze, I've been able to find out who I am and what I want from life, and the small, apparently insignificant things that always fell below my radar have leapt up and grabbed me. I have felt what it is to be alive. I've loved with my whole heart. I have experienced true living, free from anything artificial that encumbers the person I am. I've stopped being frightened of reaching out to the things I want and believe in, and I am able to bond properly with people, something I rarely did as a drinker. The old me was terrified of being found out, scared of people realising that I was unable to control how much I drank.

What a terrible waste it is to spend life cowering in fear, sidestepping the beauty, excitement and wonder that are at our fingertips simply because we are too scared to test the alcohol-free water. The X-factor that we are seeking is really just life, but life in all its simplicity as opposed to the artificial version that alcohol serves up. It arises when we are truly able to tap into our authentic self, comfortable in being who we are and able to communicate with other people in an honest and real way.

When you quit drinking, there is a danger that the void alcohol leaves behind won't be filled quickly enough, and you'll seek out that perceived sense of excitement and wonder once more from the bottle. But your X-factor won't arrive on your doorstep overnight, and it won't happen until you've changed inside. It's necessary to go through the mill and fight against the challenges that previously you've always met with a drinking session. You need to feel the pain and be brave, dig deep and show yourself that you are, in actual fact, a strong person. You need to unearth the evidence that you can survive and you don't need to be scared at all. Only when you have walked this mire of emotional agony and reappeared tough and full of self-belief will you find your X-factor. And it's that which will keep you sober. Because once you've found it, you'll never want to let it go.

Y

Years: My Decades of Drinking

Teens

Teenagers develop a taste for drinking because – well – why exactly *do* they routinely develop such enthusiasm for alcohol? For a start, there are physiological reasons pertaining to human neurochemistry which is set up during adolescence to allow for intense learning. The outcome of this is the frequently passionate behaviours we witness in teenagers, with their overt desires to change the world and indulge in all kinds of exciting new activities. But this passion frequently overflows into less desirable activities too, such as alcohol use and other drug taking.

There are also the effects of parental drinking. Children learn from their parents to a greater degree than from anyone else, and so if Mum and Dad are downing multiple bottles of wine during the week to help them cope with stress and every other emotion, this will certainly become the norm within the family unit. And while the British seem to possess a deeply entrenched belief in the benefits of introducing their offspring to booze (*a la* our French neighbours), evidence would suggest that the younger a person begins to drink alcohol, the more they risk growing up to be a dependent drinker. From a purely personal perspective on this, my early introduction to wine at around the age of eight or nine (a thimbleful with Sunday dinner) did absolutely nothing to suppress my urge to get stuck into boozing once I hit my early teens.

Mortality is not a concept that most teens can relate to; the fears that begin to creep in once we hit our thirties and forties are uniformly amiss in youth. This is another factor in the propensity of the young to engage in binge-drinking. The health harms of alcohol use do not seem applicable or relevant in any way to adolescents who generally believe they will live for ever. For this reason, it can be exceptionally difficult to affect positively the way a young person thinks in terms of behaviours or activities that are bad for them.

In addition, you would have to spend your primary two decades living beneath a rock in order not to be influenced by the world of alcohol advertising and marketing. There are so many heinous examples of big alcohol firms specifically targeting the young nowadays – especially via social media – that it's difficult to know where to start on this topic. For example, on Twitter, WKD uses the following bio: 'Tweet, sleep, rave, retweet. If you're over 18!', and the company's feed is bursting with references to Beyoncé, UK premier league football clubs, fashionable beauty ideas and alcohol-sponsored dance festivals – all things deliberately aimed at the youth market. Even WKD's Twitter bio appeals directly to the under-eighteens owing to its caveat that followers must be officially adults. (Remember how the teen magazine *Just Seventeen* was wildly appealing when you were thirteen but somehow lost its edge once you actually reached the age emblazoned across its cover?) The language employed by WKD is also designed to reach a younger audience, with tweets such as 'Nights out are about to get even hotter, look out for our new WKD Shot coming soon! Perfect 4 sharing with ur mates' as standard. WKD, along with other popular alcohol brands, has perfected the art of purporting to adhere to government guidelines about alcohol advertising and marketing while establishing itself in a populist role guaranteed to attract the attention of the youth market.

It's a strategy that anyone young in the pre-social media era didn't have to contend with, but such insidious marketing is definitely now an effective means of securing new customers in this age of the ubiquitous mobile phone.

When I was a teenager during the late eighties/early nineties, it was the bands I listened to, the films I watched and an unfathomable something else that influenced me in terms of my desire to drink. That unknown factor was anchored in a deeply felt sense of naughtiness. I wanted to be bad, and alcohol, with its concrete alliance with rebellion, was so obvious to me as the answer that I never wondered for one single minute about not taking up with it. When I started drinking aged thirteen, it felt like coming home – as if I'd discovered a missing part of me after years spent achingly empty inside.

As we develop from children to adults, we are frequently beset by insecurities and a desperate wish to fit in and conform. It's this intrinsic vulnerability that is so readily resolved with alcohol, the magic formula that regulates all our differences, blasts our fragile forms into the realm of supremely confident cool kids and helps alleviate every unique social awkwardness experienced in the agonising years of young adulthood. And by the time we've passed our teen years, we are locked into a habit that is (or so it would seem) almost impossible to break.

Twenties

I was married at twenty-three and a mum at the same age. I felt like a grown-up, but looking back now from the perspective of a forty-year-old, I appreciate that I was far from it. I was playing at being an adult, and the drinking I engaged in was merely tweaked as I saw fit for my new role. I definitely did not magically switch to responsible drinking once I'd waved goodbye to my teenage years.

Just as every other commodity out there is tailored to its target audience – think beauty products aimed at teenagers (energising, fresh and invigorating formulas) versus those directed at older women (firming and repairing creams, age-defence technology) – alcoholic drinks are marketed specifically at the individuals companies hope will buy them. I drank pints of bitter and lager during my teens, but by my mid-twenties it was white wine all the way. Wine, it was decreed by someone in the world of alcohol sales, was sophisticated and a treat, not a beverage consumed by desperately dependent boozers seeking a socially acceptable means of getting wasted. Cultural signifiers abounded during the latter part of the twentieth century and early years of the new millennium hailing wine as a feminine, glamorous drink, with its champions ranging from Bridget Jones to the cast of *Sex and the City*. Women everywhere, or so it appeared, were getting sloshed on wine and loving every minute of it.

In our twenties we are still not quite adults, especially those of us who have consistently leaned too heavily upon alcohol as an emotional prop. The approval of our peers continues to be all-important and we're somewhat unsure of freely revealing the person we are inside.

During this decade, I was aware of a powerful tribal need that governed my social tendencies, compelling me to *belong*. I was rarely alone; many of my days were spent hanging out with other mums and our children, and the nights were occasions to drink – either with friends, my then-husband, or both. Old photos from my twenties almost exclusively feature me among big groups of people, all laughing and joking and drinking. My friends and I held parties on a regular basis, and when we weren't partying we were in bars or restaurants, consuming alcohol there instead. We were not prepared to discard the hedonism of our teens, despite all of us being parents by this stage. But oddly, I don't recall a single acquaintance from that period in my life raising the issue of alcohol being problematic – even after the night I slipped into an unconscious state on the kitchen table midway through a party and remained there until dawn like a slab of meat. It's just drinking; it's what we do…

I had self-esteem issues at this age as, I imagine, most people do. The wisdom and self-belief that we obtain with age is not usually on the radar prior to people turning thirty (at least). At a time in life when we are presented with an abundance of grown-up activities for the first time ever – house buying, having children, establishing proper careers – alcohol is omnipresent. It flows freely at weddings (our own and those of friends) and work events, and is a staple of sophisticated dinner parties. Pubs have long since stopped being the forbidden and naughty places they were during our teenage years, having become havens of social bonding instead. And the combination of still-lacking self-confidence and culturally normalised drinking marks out the twenties as a decade of pure alcoholic indulgence for a large percentage of the population.

We also do not usually experience hangovers of quite such potency in our younger years as we do post-thirty, which certainly helps in keeping the booze flowing.

In the midst of my twenties, I was far more sexually conscious than I am now, aged forty. I loved dressing up, going out and attracting male glances –

even after I was married. I never pursued any such attention as a married woman, but it was a driver in my zesty passion for socialising. And guess what? Alcohol and sexual awareness together is a match made in heaven ... or so it feels. Looking back, the nights in sweaty clubs, the evenings in bars, the wedding receptions and the birthday parties – so many were coloured by my interest in the opposite sex. Drinking had been long established as an enabler in this respect – booze plus me equated to feelings of sexiness and being lusted after (even if in reality I was often appearing drunk and not at all attractive to anyone). Nights out with friends in the town centre comprised a lesser version of female holidays abroad which, pre-marriage, were an excuse for heavy drinking and mingling as much as possible with the opposite sex.

During my twenties, although tinged with the awfulness of my divorce towards the latter end of the decade, booze was mostly fun. Yes, I drank far too much, and there were some instances of which I am definitely not proud, but there were some good times. And by the time I was fast approaching my thirties, I was desperate to hang on to those happy days – perhaps not realising that I couldn't.

Thirties

I do regard my thirties with great affection, for it was the decade in which I grew up, and the one in which I stopped drinking. It started out pretty terribly, a hangover from my turbulent, wild twenties characterised almost solely by my single parent status and all the associated problems I struggled with. I had no idea who I was, and even though I acknowledged that many of my lifestyle choices were having a negative impact on my mental health and life generally, I was clueless about what I needed to do in order to turn things around.

There were a couple of significant relationships, both founded upon a river of booze. There was a stab at a better career – a law degree as a mature student followed by deep depression because the glittering legal positions didn't materialise. There was a lot of booze, and some utterly dark, shameful and frightening episodes involving nights of no control and consequential suicidal desires.

And then, aged thirty-five, in April, almost exactly halfway through my thirties, I put myself in hospital through drinking wine.

Mortality starts to creep up on most of us during these middling years, and certainly I had been experiencing an acceleration of moments of absolute clarity during which I fully accepted that I would not live for ever after all. As I was downing wine in great quantities and smoking quite a lot too, this understanding of my inevitable demise caused me to worry. With startling brutality I began to picture myself as an observer might, and those deluded notions I'd carried around with me for several years about my charm, wit and overall party animal-ness were suddenly trampled on with fervour. I didn't like what I saw, and I didn't want it to be all that I ever amounted to being.

With the booze finally gone, I allowed myself the opportunity to breathe and take in my reality for the first time ever as a grown-up. In our thirties, there is a tendency to pursue the answers to some deep questions far more than in our younger years. What is the meaning of life? Why am I here? I began to contemplate these queries, and I strongly suspect the fact that I no longer drank helped me to arrive at some acceptable conclusions. I got to know myself in my thirties and learnt to love myself – proper self-compassion, not the narcissistic and shallow self-obsession that defined me as a younger person.

Now when I regard other people consuming alcohol to excess in their thirties and beyond, I often wonder if a major motivator for their continued drinking lies in an effort to hang on to their youth. I am pretty sure that, had I not quit alcohol when I did, I would still be trapped in that cycle of boozing to feel young and attractive, followed by days of excessive self-loathing and shame because it's impossible to laugh drunkenness off when we are older. Plus, hangovers get worse with age, as do the outward physical effects of heavy drinking. And the stigma linked to older people drinking to excess is often worse than that of younger people … and on and on.

It strikes me that drinking too much will never lead us to long-lasting and true contentment, but the social fallout from drinking when we are older is weightier than in our younger years. Which is why drinking too much in our thirties can often slide into the murky realm of secret boozing behind closed doors.

Forties

The forties is a decade when physically the ageing process becomes more noticeable. I'll be forty-one later this year, and for the first time in my life I've found myself climbing the stairs like a tired old dog last thing at night. My knees creak a bit these days too, and the facial creases and wrinkles that I'd hoped might give me a wide berth have now found permanent residency upon my brow and around my eyes. And not wishing to focus too strongly on the downsides of this age (because there are *loads* of positives), most of us find that we no longer have the body we (probably) took for granted in our twenties.

Women in particular can be subjected to huge pressures around this time in our lives, aware as most of us are of the disparaging societal assessment that we are now beyond our prime. It can be challenging, to say the least, to be perpetually bombarded by a standardised version of beautiful (i.e. white twenty-something blonde with long legs and a tiny waist) which it is nigh on impossible to live up to. The forties is also a time when many women find themselves with children growing up and flying the nest, which further adds to feelings of redundancy and ageing.

And in our forties, we are most definitely not deemed to be of an age when public drunkenness is

OK, which, when combined with the above, makes this a time when drinking at home appears a safer bet all round. It's a means to forget that we are no longer young and quite so needed, all done away from prying eyes. There are life events unfolding for many people during their forties (divorce, children leaving home, major job dissatisfaction and a general perplexity as to what the point is to everything) which lend themselves to an increased wish to escape. Alcohol, of course, for the lifetime drinker provides the obvious respite.

As a woman who has entered her forties a non-drinker for five years, I would like to point out that I have never felt happier or more mentally resilient than I do right now. I take care of my body and, while it's not quite what it was at the age of twenty, it's not that different. In some respects, I'm in much better shape (I have never had toned arms before now), and in terms of my diet and overall wellbeing, I am the healthiest I have ever been. I'm pragmatic and rational, and I've beaten the ongoing depression that plagued me intermittently throughout my drinking years.

I do accept the downsides to life and the occasional pointlessness of it, and the fact that some people don't like me, and that on certain days it's grey and rubbish and I just want to lie in bed and do nothing, but nowhere among these less-than-cheerful moments is a desire to drink. I am sure that drinking never works as a means of improving our situation, and certainly not when it comes to halting our advancing years. Far better to acquire wisdom and gratitude; to devote our time to new interests and passions; to slow down the physical impact of ageing by leading a healthy, alcohol-free life so that we're happy we look and feel our best; to enjoy the mental calm and positivity that come so naturally with looking after our physical selves. All of this is possible, and it's found on the other side of alcohol dependency in a place of wellness and acceptance of the ageing process.

These are the decades of drinking of which I have personal experience, and I see common threads running through people of these age groups on Soberistas. There are, of course, many people who quit drinking when in their fifties and beyond, and their reasons for doing so, although varied, can be equally similar. It is *never* too late to stop drinking and allow yourself the opportunity to live life with clarity, freed from the foggy blinkers of alcohol. The health benefits of putting an end to years of binge-drinking are vast, no matter what age we are at when we finally put down the bottle.

Z

Zzzzzzz – Sleep When You Are Sober

Alcohol is both the giver and the thief when it comes to sleep. How tempting it can be to down a few glasses of booze during the evening knowing that sleep will almost certainly follow, and when it does it will be akin to sliding into a coma. However, as any binge-drinker will testify, fast-forward a few hours and the alcohol will cause you to snap wide-awake, complete with a dry, furry mouth, pounding heart rate and the headache from hell. And to make matters worse, the sleep you secured prior to that point will not have been of quality because alcohol robs people of REM (rapid eye movement) and the deeper, restorative stages of sleep.

I've experienced several episodes of insomnia during my adult years, and I know that (especially during my twenties) I used alcohol as a means of knocking myself out. Insomnia is awful, and even booze-induced sleep, with its diminished benefits, is preferable to lying awake all night, staring at the ceiling and panicking over all the things you need to do the next day on zero shuteye.

When I was aged twenty, a man with whom I'd

recently been in a relationship attacked me, waking me up as I lay in bed by holding a hammer to my face. The incident was horrific and scarred me intensely, and for many years I was petrified of being alone in a house at night. Rather than sit with the fear and dread that the attack had instilled within me, I opted to drink a lot of wine whenever I found myself unaccompanied in the evenings. It developed into a habit very quickly, and I justified it to myself as being the result of the severity of the attack. Of my two options – being stone cold sober, filled with abject terror at every creaking radiator, every car driving past, every unexplained sound in the house, or anaesthetising myself against such anxieties with a couple of bottles of wine – I picked the booze unequivocally every time.

It took more than ten years to break this habit, and it's only since I stopped drinking completely that I can say categorically I am fine with being in a house alone at night. At first, without alcohol numbing me, I was forced to endure the fear, just as I would have done all those years earlier had I dealt with it when sober. But gradually, as I grew acquainted with my in-built sense of safety, I learnt to trust myself. I employed the strategy of thinking of the worst possible outcomes (intruder tries to break in with weapon intending to attack me, for example) and then visualising my response. Without alcohol in my system, I would be able to hear properly, being more alert to any strange sounds and reactive in my responses.

I also contemplated my survival chances

generally, and found comfort in reasoning that my number could, realistically, be up at any time – crossing a road, driving down the motorway or shopping in town. When it happens I would rather be sober and with clarity, enjoying my life free from the shackles of alcohol dependency and not pissed out of my head. Alcohol would not prevent anyone from breaking into my house, but it would severely hamper my ability to protect myself should it ever occur again.

We can suffer insomnia for any reason and at any time during our lives. As well as the aforementioned example, I have experienced it during pregnancy, amid the breakdown of relationships and when I have been living with stress arising from a number of different situations. I've taken sleeping tablets and antidepressants, and I have utilised alcohol on many nights purely as a method of falling asleep.

When people stop drinking, it is often with the assumption that the quality of their sleep will suddenly miraculously improve. However, it's not always the case (as with weight loss) that this happens overnight. There can be underlying issues contributing to bouts of insomnia (depression or bereavement, for instance), physical symptoms of withdrawal (the impact of abruptly quitting drinking after sustained alcohol misuse can be very unpleasant, including sweating, nausea, headaches and loss of appetite) to contend with, and anxiety and fear surrounding both your alcohol misuse and how you will cope with life without booze.

This terror of facing daily existence in all its

facets without the old crutch of alcohol is very real. For regular drinkers who rely on booze across the patchwork of problems life throws their way, to be confronted with any of them sober can be truly daunting – and sleeping is routinely one of the worst in this respect.

As with much of the process of becoming happily alcohol-free, learning to sleep sober can take time, so the first thing to remind yourself of here is to be patient. By putting pressure on yourself to begin sleeping soundly every night as soon as you've quit drinking, you will only increase the difficulties in achieving this.

Much of the advice for establishing a good bedtime routine you will no doubt already be familiar with, but it's worth emphasising it because it really does help. The primary action I would recommend is to cut out caffeine completely from lunchtime onwards – that's no dark chocolate, no fizzy caffeinated drinks like cola, and definitely no coffee or tea. Next up, my old favourite: exercise! Research suggests that when we engage in any physical activity that raises the heart rate for about thirty minutes (brisk walking, jogging, riding a bike, swimming, playing football in the garden with the kids), we are likely to sleep more deeply and soundly – fatigue the mind and body, and the need for sleep increases. My personal experience would certainly support these findings, as when I haven't exercised for a few days I most definitely notice a lack of sleep quality and an increased difficulty in dropping off. (Just remember that you might need to exercise for around four months before noticing an improvement in sleep, so again, be patient and don't expect miracles overnight.)

Don't go to sleep during the day, and regulate sleeping patterns so that you generally get up and go to bed at the same times each day.

A warm bath with scented candles and dim lights, followed by dressing in comfy pyjamas, is a sure fire means of preparing yourself mentally for sleep. Put some thought into the state of your bedroom in the evenings, too – it shouldn't be too hot or too cold, and should be free from draughts. And it might seem like a silly thing, but investing in some luxurious bed linen, a pretty bedside lamp (keep the light subdued at all times) and some new pillows can all be of benefit. Another crucial adjustment to make if you haven't already done so is to avoid looking at your mobile phone or tablet once you're in bed. The bright screen has the effect of keeping the mind alert. It's a far better idea to develop a habit of reading a book in soft light, instead.

Finally, introduce some basic relaxation techniques just before you try and sleep. Lie down with your eyes closed and take some deep, slow breaths – in through the nostrils and out through the mouth. Focus your attention on all of the different muscle groups in the body, one at a time and beginning with the toes. Tense the toes, then relax them fully. Repeat this all the way up through the legs, the arms and to the top of your head. Once you've achieved a relaxed state of calm, visualise somewhere peaceful and pleasant – maybe an event you are looking forward to, or a completely make-believe situation such as lying on a tropical sandy beach with your toes immersed in the warm, tranquil ocean. Concentrate on this image and continue to practise the deep breathing.

I quickly fell in love with bedtimes after I had embarked on my new alcohol-free life. There really is no comparison (once you've got the sleep thing nailed) between booze-fuelled stumbling into bed, semi-conscious and waking a few hours later with a sandpaper tongue and a ton of regrets, and calm, relaxing slumbering in gorgeous pyjamas with a clear head full of self-compassion and happy thoughts.

There's a huge issue of fear in connection with sleeping minus alcohol for many people who are new to sober living, and this can easily become a self-fulfilling prophecy. The anxieties that begin to bubble up during the evening at the imminent attempt to sleep can soon become the very reason why sleep is impossible. In order to combat this, it's important to put into perspective just what quitting alcohol really means to you. What's the worst that can happen if you do not drink? Sit down on the floor, breathe deeply and focus on these questions: what exactly will go wrong when you do not drink? Will the world stop spinning? Will you despise yourself even more than you probably have done in the past as a result of binge-drinking? Will your friends and family decide they hate you?

No, of course not. The very worst that will happen is that you'll set out on the process of learning to live free from all the many restrictions and negative mental and bodily health harms that alcohol presents. The first few days will be the most challenging in terms of the physical effects of eliminating alcohol from your life (if you are in any doubt at all as to whether you are physically addicted to alcohol and should therefore reduce your intake gradually, visit your GP who will be able to advise you based on your individual circumstances). Once you have this early phase out of the way, it's all about throwing yourself into getting happy and well again, and by utilising all the advice in this book – which comes from the heart and is based on my own alcohol-free journey – you will hopefully find it nowhere near as scary as you might have imagined it to be.

Good luck, sweet dreams, and I hope you enjoy your new alcohol-free life as much as I love mine.

Lucy Rocca x

A sample chapter of

THE SOBER REVOLUTION

by Sarah Turner and Lucy Rocca

Available now from Accent Press

Introduction
by Lucy Rocca

As she described to me the events of one particular night which had, like many others before it, descended into a drunken mess of staggering, screaming, self-pity and the subsequent stomach-lurching moments the morning after when, upon waking, the staccato memories had risen to the surface and she recalled some (definitely not all – the blackouts were always severe) of the terrible things she had said and done, Carol's voice was full of sad resignation. It was as though she was describing another person's life, someone whom she loved and cared for deeply but who she hadn't seen in a long time.

The summer barbeque had started out like any other; friends and family gathered for an afternoon of relaxation, good food and a few drinks in the warm sunshine. Carol, who in her own words was a greedy drunk, felt from the moment she arrived that there was only one real reason she was in attendance at this friend's convivial get-together, and it came in three colours – red, white, and rosé. Mingling amongst her friends, enjoying their company as well as the sensation of becoming slightly tipsy, Carol continued to fill her glass, gradually losing track of how much she'd had.

Unsure of when or how things suddenly switched in her head, she was told the next day how she had, after consuming many large glasses of wine, launched into tirades and abusive diatribes aimed at anyone and everyone around her. Descending into a wild and drunken rage, Carol was eventually bundled into the car with her husband and two boys and carted off back home where she could sleep it off. Upon reaching the house, however, sleep was the last thing on her mind and before long the neighbours felt justified in calling the police, concerned over the fact that Carol's two young sons were present in what appeared to be a domestic situation that was spinning rapidly out of all control.

In the mid-1990s when the barbecue incident occurred amidst numerous other regrettable drunken events, Carol was in her early thirties, mum of two sons, and caught in a marriage that was heading to an unhappy close. Her successful career placed tough demands on her which, together with the juggling of her home life and the doomed relationship which would soon end in bitter divorce, resulted in an ever-increasing affection for the wine.

As I spoke to Carol about her experiences just a few weeks before the completion of this book, it was eminently clear that I was in conversation with an articulate, confident, and sensible woman who doted on her family and valued her life, and all those who featured in it, highly. This is someone, now in her early fifties, who has recently taken up martial arts, embarked on a counselling course, has lost three stone, looks the best she has in decades and is bursting with optimism and hope for the future.

Carol's story of alcohol dependency is one which is not, sadly, uncommon. Launching into a drinking career in her twenties which took a sharp turn for the worse a decade down the line when her marriage hit the rocks and she was faced with the crippling loneliness and hardship which result from a difficult and acrimonious divorce, Carol was never a woman who could 'just have one.' As soon as the cork was popped she had her eye on what was left – would there be enough? What if it ran out? Could she justify a trip to the shop for some other imagined necessity which would enable her to slip an extra bottle into the supermarket basket – oh, so innocently, just like everyone else does?

Holding down a demanding job in which she managed hundreds of people, Carol desperately fought to maintain the façade of the 'she can have it all' 1980s mantra to friends and family. She was the life and soul, the consummate party girl, who every so often went too far and fell over the precipice into drunk and out of control.

For many who find themselves caught up in the vicious grip of an alcohol dependency, the denial is so much a part of what they are living through that it is all too easy to imagine there are no real problems caused by their drinking to excess. It is ever tempting to point at others and berate their immoral lifestyle and the effect it has on them and their families, while simultaneously wrapping ourselves in a blanket of pretence and ignoring what we are doing to our own little worlds.

As the years progressed and her drinking increased (along with the associated traumas), Carol did become aware of the impact her alcohol use may have been having on her sons.

The self-hatred and inner torment she experienced as a result of each and every awful episode fuelled by drinking led to the further erosion of Carol's inner strength and the faculties she needed so badly to sober up and dig her way out of the hole she was sinking into.

Carol did eventually put the brakes on and stopped drinking alcohol for good just over a year ago. The awful accumulation of drunken arguments, loss of self-respect, hurtful comments made which seemed to have been spoken by someone outside of her and which often she could not remember the next day, falling over, unexplained bruises, embarrassing herself in a myriad of different ways, and not being the person who she knew she was capable of being inside, eventually became too much. Carol had never descended so low as to lose her home, be disowned by her family, or sacked from her job because of her dependency on alcohol, but twenty long years of drunkenness left its scars.

For a couple of months following her bold decision to take control of her life and eradicate alcohol completely from it, Carol's relationships with her two now grown up sons improved dramatically. Both were impressed by their mum's ability to find herself amongst the wreckage of alcohol abuse, and her new upbeat mood and increased interest in their lives as opposed to being permanently side-tracked by wondering where the next glass was coming from, helped the three of them enjoy a closeness that had been missing for a while.

Last September, just a couple of months after Carol drank her last alcoholic drink, her eldest son died suddenly, aged twenty-eight. Resulting from an accidental overdose of the prescription drug Zomorph, his death came out of the blue and was horribly shocking. As I spoke to Carol about the tragedy of losing her son, I was struck by her unfaltering strength and the incredibly brave and dignified way in which she has since held the rest of the family together and remained intact for their benefit. Understanding how much it had meant to her son that she had finally managed to conquer her demons and put down the bottle, Carol explained to me how so much of her motivation for living positively and healthily now, originated in words he spoke to her just days before the end of his life; "*Mum, you not drinking is a very good thing.*"

Carol is well aware that should she resume the destructive relationship she once had with alcohol she would not be the person she is today; with her hope and courage, together with all the ample time and energy she is now able to spend on those around her, Carol's *raison d'être* is to claw back the life she lost to drinking for so many years and to give back whatever she can. Knowing that her son spent precious time with her in the final months of his life during which she was free from the grip of alcohol and all of its soul-destroying effects, gives Carol some comfort in the tragic aftermath of his death.

It has become blindingly clear to her that upon escaping the alcohol trap, the world opens up. Ruminating over the pointlessness of consuming all that wine could be enough to make a lesser person sink, but Carol has found the strength to fight, carving out a new and meaningful existence of which her son would be proud. There are no longing glances at a guest's glass of wine across the dining table, or feelings of resentment towards her hugely supportive partner for his desire to have a couple of glasses before dinner; Carol has thrown herself headlong into the wonderful world of sobriety and is relishing all the positivity that it has introduced into her life.

Fully aware of the fact that sobriety is an all or nothing prize, of the impossibility of reaping the many rewards that are derived from an alcohol-free life without committing to it one hundred per cent, Carol is in this for the long haul.

Looking back over her lifetime, she is now able to extract the good and employ it as the foundations for even better, while simultaneously accepting she will never change what's been and gone. The wonderfully positive characteristics that emanate from Carol, despite all she has faced in the last twelve months, are what led me to asking her if I could share her story for the purpose of this introduction. In my opinion, she embodies all that it is to love life, in control.

Carol is one of many women who unwittingly slip into the realms of alcohol dependency, so busy with attempting to keep the many plates of their lives spinning that they fail to notice how the pleasant glass of wine after the kids have been put to bed slowly transforms into a much-needed crutch, longingly lusted after throughout each and every hectic day. People who wind up with a 'drinking problem' are, for the most part, a long way off the archetypal drunk sleeping on a park bench with an oversized bottle of cheap cider to hand. Those who struggle with an alcohol dependency are everyday people who once 'enjoyed a drink' but for whom gradually the alluring qualities of booze are replaced by something much more sinister.

Pigeon-holing very heavy drinkers as 'alcoholics' is an easy way to deflect the accusatory finger away from one's own destructive relationship with booze – *'I never drink before tea-time'* and *'I never touch spirits'* being commonly used reassurances which prevent people from facing up to the fact that they are, in actual fact, alcohol-dependent.

Because I never considered myself to be 'an alcoholic' I failed to pay much attention to how dangerously unhealthy my wine habit had become. My daughter was never under threat of being taken into care, I had a nice place to live and was never in a position where I couldn't pay the mortgage, and I still looked reasonably OK, as the really obvious visible signposting of physical damage caused by excessive alcohol consumption becomes far more apparent further down the line. I stopped drinking alcohol aged thirty-five, and had only recently begun to notice during the previous couple of years the more prominent and difficult-to-hide facial indicators of being hung-over; the ruddy complexion, sallow skin, sunken eyes and overly red lips becoming regular features of my appearance as my drinking reached epic proportions.

At my worst I was consuming around one hundred and fifty units per week, which equates to one or two bottles of wine a night with a few extra drinks thrown in at the weekend. Even then, I did not feel constantly alarmed at the amount I was drinking – rather I was occasionally beset (usually upon waking in the middle of the night) by a terribly morbid fear that I was killing myself slowly, and that any day I would find a lump somewhere on my person, the indicator of a lifestyle-induced cancer. But for the most part I threw caution to the wind and continued apace with socialising, boozing, and living in denial.

I consumed my last drink in April 2011, and since then have rediscovered the person I am. It is only with complete sobriety that I have come to realise just how much of the real me I sacrificed in exchange for alcohol.

I grew up wanting to be a writer. I loved reading and ploughed my way through *Watership Down* and *Jane Eyre* before I reached my teens. Scattered amongst the belongings in my bedroom were scores of notebooks filled with scribbles and doodles, little ideas for stories that popped into my head constantly. It never occurred to me that I wouldn't one day write a book or become a journalist when I grew up.

And then I discovered drinking. Alcohol had many negative effects on my life during the twenty years in which I consumed it excessively, but one thing it robbed me of which I am especially grateful to have rediscovered as a result of becoming alcohol-free, is my creativity. It is only with sober hindsight that I can truly appreciate just how barren my life had become as a result of my on-going drunkenness, where the only interest I had outside of my family and job was drinking.

Living in the UK and growing up amongst a culture which positively celebrates alcohol, spending my weekends inebriated was a completely expected part of life, and I never imagined for a moment that I would not jump on board the drunken merry-go-round along with everyone else. My friends all drank regularly, boyfriends were always heavy drinkers and so I found myself easily drawn into a habit of emotional and mental alcohol dependence which was, unfortunately, to last for two decades.

At the time of writing I have not touched alcohol for twenty-six months and I have never been happier, more positive or so full of self-confidence, more productive, a better and more capable mother or in such good physical shape. In a relatively short space of time my life has completely turned around and I owe it to the simple act of choosing to not drink alcohol.

Shortly after Soberistas.com was launched in November 2012, I was contacted by an addiction counsellor and cognitive behavioural therapist called Sarah Turner. After successfully turning her own life around after years of abusing alcohol, Sarah retrained and became a qualified practitioner, enabling her to establish the Harrogate Sanctuary in 2006 which offers women a guiding light out of the gloom of alcohol addiction. Sarah read about Soberistas in a newspaper and recognised immediately that we both had a keen desire to offer help and support to the same demographic; grown-up women who had hit the bottle hard in their efforts to cope with life's struggles.

A few months after our initial meeting Sarah and I agreed upon the idea of putting a book together that would offer practical help for beating an alcohol dependency, based on our own personal experiences. Our collaboration would be much more than a standard self-help book, however, in that it would also include real life case studies of women (and one of a married couple) who have battled their demons and emerged out of the other side shining. The sense of optimism and inspiration that can be derived from reading about people who once felt deeply unhappy and desperate as a consequence of alcohol but who, through a variety of different methods eventually resolved their difficulties, can be vast and incredibly motivating.

Sarah and I both perceive our troubled drinking histories as akin to doomed love affairs – in our efforts to acquire self-confidence and be loved and comforted, we increasingly turned to the bottle hoping the hollowness in our lives could somehow be filled by the liquid inside. Drinking and getting drunk perpetually for years, the drawn out battles we were engaged in with alcohol were not dissimilar to some of the unsatisfactory love affairs with men that marked our late teens and early twenties. As the relationship progressed, the booze took more and more and we lost all sense of our identities, emotional strength, and the ability to walk away. Alcohol gradually transformed the both of us from strong and feisty women who knew exactly what we wanted from life, to a pair of weak-willed, powerless nobodies whose only care in the world was where the next drink was coming from.

For me, coming of age during the 'ladette' years when it was suddenly de rigueur to neck pints on a night out in an effort to keep up with the lads, meant that my lack of awareness in recognising when I'd had enough to drink, and my desire to consume alcohol to the point of collapse, both went largely unnoticed. I simply blended in with a social group of hedonistic boozers who thought absolutely nothing of drinking for twelve hours straight.

It was many years later before I came to notice that the people around me no longer appeared to spend their entire weekends getting sloshed, and for most, being seen to be blatantly drunk was an embarrassment that they would attempt to avoid at all costs. Despite the awareness that I grew to have of people generally frowning on those who fall out of taxis blind drunk, engage in loud nonsensical arguments in the street or throw up loudly in a pub toilet, slumped on the floor and hanging onto the porcelain for dear life, I still maintained my reputation as something of 'a liability' on a night out.

Try as I might to instil some rules with regards to the amount or type of drink that I consumed, I pretty much always ended up absolutely plastered, my memory blacked out, and nothing but self-hatred and regrets the morning after. Despite years of trying, I never managed to moderate my alcohol consumption, and eventually arrived at the conclusion that for me, it was all or nothing. I chose nothing, which in the event has turned out to be my all.

I succeeded, as did Sarah, at conquering my alcohol addiction because I ultimately accepted the truth that if the agony of destructive drinking can ever come to an end, it has to be replaced by a solid commitment to *not drinking*. Obvious as that may sound, many people reach the decision that their relationship with alcohol is unhealthy and must be addressed, that they no longer wish to suffer all the associated awfulness of regular binge drinking, while simultaneously hoping against hope that somehow they will be able to manage their problem through control and moderation.

The vast number of people who have wiped out years of their lives through the misguided belief that alcohol is serving a purpose (stress reliever, relaxant, mood enhancer) when in actuality it is responsible for robbing them of their self-confidence, self-esteem, happiness and ability to view the world unhampered by blinkers, is staggering. For so many, the fact that they have yet to characterise themselves as 'an alcoholic' because they have not lost their worldly possessions or resorted to sleeping on a park bench means they allow themselves to spin out the delusion a little while longer – that they are in control of alcohol and not the other way around.

Adopting a lifestyle of sobriety restores the mind and body to what they once were, and allows us to fill the shoes of the person we were born to be. Making the choice to stop drinking alcohol means empowering one's self; taking charge of one's own life and ensuring a much greater degree of emotional stability, which will impact positively on those closest to us. Ditching the demon drink means walking away from the endless cycle of negativity and bashing of self – the mornings filled with recriminations and self-hatred, when the only option appears to be hiding under the duvet and wishing the world would disappear, will vanish without a trace, never to be seen again.

In writing this book we have no desire to appear evangelical, and recognise that there are many people in this world who enjoy a drink and are able to have fun with it. However, our intention is to show that life is not the boring and dull existence so often portrayed by society when depicting those who choose to not drink alcohol. Just as drunks are stigmatized, often so are non-drinkers; they are frequently considered odd, perhaps once weak-minded or unable to let their hair down, rather than people who are in control and able to fulfil their true potential.

Throughout the following chapters you will read the remarkable stories of women who eventually arrived at the conclusion that a life minus alcohol had to be better than the continuation of the booze-inflicted misery in which they had been drowning for so long. Despite, for all, an initial terror at the prospect of a life spent separated from their one true love, alcohol, all nine of the case studies ultimately arrived at the conclusion that they only really embarked upon the act of living once the wine had been kicked out of their lives for good. Seven of the women whose stories are featured in this book are previous clients of Sarah who kindly, and very bravely, agreed to Sarah writing up her case notes on each of them, in order to create a powerful collection of real life recovery tales.

During the 1990s, feminism for me was best illustrated by the fact that women could happily prop up the bar next to any number of men and smoke and drink pints with them all evening. Now in my late thirties, I consider alcohol to be the key factor in the transformation of my personality from strong and full of gumption in my teens, to depressed, anxiety-ridden, and severely lacking in self-confidence and self-belief by my early thirties – a fine example of anti-feminism.

The love/hate relationship that so many people endure with alcohol is surely nothing but the antithesis to nurturing a happy existence in which we fulfil our potential and maximise the opportunities which surround us from the moment we are born. Becoming dependent on alcohol leads to a dead end; a horribly predictable negative cycle where nothing ever improves and the same mistakes are made over and over again.

In writing this book, Sarah and I set out to describe a mind-set which we believe is the key to successfully walking away from a destructive relationship with alcohol. By fully acknowledging the fact that alcohol adds nothing to your life and is actually responsible for preventing you from reaching self-fulfilment, it *is* possible to break the long-standing drinking patterns that become so innocuously entrenched in our lives.

If one embarks on alcohol-free living with the deep-seated belief that they've given up something of worth then they are heading for a resounding fall from the wagon. To conquer alcohol-dependency, it is crucial never to consider one's self to be '*on the wagon*' in the first place; this expression is loaded with connotations of temporariness, a short-term quiescence from normal life. In order to walk away from booze for good, it is essential that upon reaching this incredibly positive and empowering decision, you recognise that it is a step which will lead you to great things, the beginning of an exciting adventure and a whole new way of life.

What you are NOT doing is giving up a treat and choosing to live your life like a hermit who can have no fun; you are resurrecting the old you from the wasteland of drink-fuelled misery and discovering what the world is really about, minus the booze blinkers that have kept you submerged for so long.

This book came about as a result of both Sarah's and my perception of our erstwhile relationships with alcohol being similar in many ways to doomed love affairs, and because we believe that becoming alcohol-free is a lifestyle choice that demands commitment right from the start. There will be bad days and good days (over time the good most definitely outweigh the bad), rocky patches and feelings of doubt, but ultimately, empowering yourself by ditching alcohol can only come about if you stick with your decision.

In this way we believe that committing to sobriety resembles, in many ways, the personal investment many people put into a long-term relationship.

Imagine finding a partner who makes you feel wonderful every day – who boosts your self-esteem, makes you feel confident and self-assured, is financially stable, fires up your passion for life, encourages your productivity, supports your endeavours to be a great parent, pampers you, encourages you to take good care of yourself by eating the right foods and exercising, and guides you along a path of self-discovery.

This person would nurture your character, never trying to sway you to be someone you aren't. He would make you see that you are uniquely perfect, someone to be cherished and celebrated. He would acknowledge your flaws but accept and love them as a part of you, as imperfections of a perfect one-off – you.

If you could drop yourself into a world in which this person not only exists but is also ready and waiting for you to be by his side for ever, would you contemplate making a commitment to him? If all of the above was guaranteed to be yours for as long as you were prepared to stay true to our imaginary Mr Wonderful, would you make the leap of faith and say yes?

In this book you will read about a lifestyle choice

that is simple to make, relatively easy to stick to and guaranteed to provide you with the tools required for a real and positive state of being. It's a choice that you may have dabbled with the idea of for years, never quite knowing whether to make the final leap, or perhaps it's something that you have only recently been considering. Either way, if you continue to read on, you will find out that the choice of sobriety is the lifestyle equivalent of our imaginary Mr Wonderful, and it is yours for the taking.

All you have to do is say YES.

We know this book can help you make the decision to quit drinking. It will help you start on a very liberating journey. Please take a moment to reflect on how you are feeling about your relationship with alcohol.

- How are you feeling right now?

- Are you worried about how much you drink?

- Have you been suffering health effects from your drinking?

- Has your relationship with family and friends been impacted by your drink?

- Is it causing you problems at work?

- Would it help your finances if you stopped spending money on alcohol?

- Are you fed up with losing control?

CHAPTER ONE
Flirting With the Notion of Sobriety

For many people, alcohol has the same draw as a particularly charming yet dangerous lover; its surface attraction beguiling a hidden hotbed of deceit, unpredictability and destruction. For all those wonderful nights spent sharing a bottle of wine with friends or a partner, nibbling on tasty finger foods by candlelight and talking amiably until the cows come home, there are a plethora of arguments, ill-advised 'romantic' trysts, wine-induced carb-fests resulting in difficult-to-shift spare tyres, mornings of recriminations and self-hatred, outrageous flirtations with people not to be flirted with, embarrassing stumbles outside crowded bars and slurred, drunken behaviour in front of the kids which demands an explanation in the morning through the fog of a hangover.

And for all of the above less than charming repercussions of excessive alcohol consumption, a little thing called denial will persistently try to work its magic, persuading you to focus on the positives and ignore the ever-increasing list of negatives in order to keep you pouring.

I began drinking in my early teens. Growing up in a middle-class family with teachers for parents, a large house in the suburbs, and the requisite black Labrador, I hailed from a secure and totally functional background. I have no particular excuses for embarking upon an exceptionally destructive relationship with wine (and beer and spirits when the wine ran dry) other than it's what teenagers did in suburban Sheffield in the late 1980s.

We loitered around the school grounds on warm summer evenings, smoking Marlboros, listening to The Smiths and drinking expensive bottles of Claret or Pinot Noir stolen from various friends' affluent parents' wine cellars. As the years passed by my friends changed in person but not in type and I continued to socialise with those who 'liked a drink.' It was therefore never forefront in my mind that I drank too much or that I (heaven forbid!) might have a dependency on booze.

In the halcyon years of my late teens and twenties, long before the idea of my own mortality had raised its gloomy head and I lived beneath a sun that apparently would never set, risks to personal health posed by fun and outrageous nights spent drinking purely to get drunk, puffing away on cigarettes with as much concern as if they were the confectionary version bought for a penny as a child, it was easy to float along, quietly developing an emotional dependency on alcohol without realising it.

Beneath my outward recklessness, however, I did read and latch onto fixedly the news stories which began to emerge in the early 1990s regarding red wine and how it allegedly had health benefits. Following the US news programme 60 Minutes airing a story entitled 'French Paradox' which highlighted the low incidence rate of heart disease amongst the French despite their love of high fat and dairy foods, pointing to their equal love of vin rouge as an explanation for this, the US saw sales of red wine jump by 44% over previous years. The story quickly found its way across the Atlantic, helping to reassure the boozy Britons that they too were being good to themselves by drinking all that alcohol.

The Mediterranean diet, all those gloriously healthy Tuscans drinking their Chianti and scoffing beans, artichokes, and olives under a baking Italian sun – somewhere in my befuddled mind I adopted the belief that I too was buying into such a life each time I dropped a nice bottle of red into my shopping trolley along with some antipasti and a selection of artisan breads.

But the fact that I was cherry-picking the positive news stories regarding drinking habits and choosing to ignore the less reassuring ones would suggest that as far back as fifteen years prior to my stopping drinking alcohol altogether, I had begun to worry about my wine habit just a little.

So what might cause you to have concerns over the amount of alcohol you are consuming? You, your friends, and partner all drink at every social event you attend, occasionally becoming inebriated, rowdy, and a little irresponsible. The hangovers have always been a constant presence since you began drinking and are therefore part and parcel of this ubiquitous and very accepted form of substance abuse that you regularly partake in, but recently they have become somewhat debilitating resulting in you spending half the weekend in bed. The panic attacks and state of paranoia that you suffer following particularly heavy drinking episodes may have become more intense and are occurring with an increased frequency, and perhaps you have begun to regularly experience memory blackouts.

Despite all of the negative consequences that occur as a direct result of the alcohol that you drink, you have most likely become something of a con artist to yourself, developing a brilliantly honed technique of denial and preferred ignorance over the years which affords you room to drink undeterred by worry. That is, until the morning after when you are plagued with the fear, depression, and sinking regrets over what you did the night before.

It is a common phenomenon that finds most regular binge drinkers clutching their head in woe on a Saturday or Sunday morning, despairing of their actions from the previous night's activities and swearing to themselves and anyone else who will listen that they will never touch the stuff again – only to repeat their actions the following weekend.

As a regular binge-drinker you will more than likely have toyed with the idea of giving up alcohol time and time again. It's an easy little plaything, one that doesn't demand any real commitment or thinking time but a fleeting thought of 'Maybe I'll stop drinking for a while.'

Imagine that alcohol is a particularly unsuitable lover who you know is no good for you. Although you recognise him as an ill match, he is charming and persuasive and despite the fact that your evenings often end in rows you can't help getting in touch with him again as soon as things blow over, your faithful return as predictable as a boomerang's. Over and over again the same pattern plays out; you meet, you have fun, you fight, you part company, you make up, you have earth-shattering sex, you cuddle, you fight, and around and around you go.

I had a relationship like this soon after my divorce in my late twenties. The man in question was as handsome as they come, we had a lot of fun, and we were very physically attracted to each other. But there the positive connections ended leaving little else to glue us together as a couple. In my head I knew I should break up with him, but the lure of him and the law of attraction kept on pulling me back for approximately a year.

Eventually I saw sense and we split up for good, but saying goodbye to him was not dissimilar to ending other addictions I have battled and eventually conquered. I had to adjust to filling my time with other things; I had to find alternative sources of comfort whenever I craved a cuddle or a boost to my flailing ego.

Many people are addicted to the drama and topsy-turvy chaos that heavy alcohol consumption brings with it – even if they don't know it. Regularly getting drunk usually means engaging in one or more of the following; messing up relationships, breaking promises, being reckless, coping with huge shame and regret, flirting with strangers, having affairs, making impetuous decisions, and acting upon whimsical, romantic notions that seem like a great idea after too many glasses of Pinot Grigio. Frequently getting sloshed is not dissimilar to being involved with a wayward and thoroughly unsuitable partner – you want him and then he lets you down, over and over again.

What starts off as an exciting union of passion and hotbed of thrills slowly dwindles into a boring, repetitive cycle of crazed pleasure-seeking, dampened swiftly by a blanket of regret.

Partners who turn out to be unsuitable do not usually reveal themselves as such in the first instance. When you initially began to drink alcohol you probably enjoyed the buzz it gave you, the sense of abandonment and possibly the feelings of sexual confidence that led you to being rather more flirtatious than usual, less shy around someone you fancied. You may have continued to experience such pleasant reactions every time you drank alcohol for quite some time, years perhaps.

Similarly, a person who eventually reveals his self to be completely not your cup of tea is usually perceived as the total opposite in the early weeks and sometimes months of the relationship. Often it is the case that we do not even recognise when someone is having a destructive and negative effect on our lives, caught up as we are in the frenetic and emotional rush of a fresh new romance. And when the day finally dawns when we do come to realise that this person who we thought was so perfect for us once upon a time is actually totally unsuitable, it can prove difficult to give them the boot and move onto someone more reliable and steady, intertwined as we are by then in a web of emotional dependencies.

Many people enjoy the excitement of a bad lover; the ups and downs, the terrible fights followed by the passionate making up are perceived as utterly worth it when we are madly in love. If you have an emotional dependency on alcohol then the thought of giving up all that recklessness, the sense of throwing caution to the wind as the first glass slips down after a long, gruelling day, the sophisticated way you feel when you sip champagne from a cut crystal flute dressed in a pretty dress and heels – relinquishing all of that for a more steady and predictable life, sober, can be a hard concept to grasp.

When we pour that first drink of the evening we are saying to those around us, "This is my time now; I'm here, but this is Mummy's wine o'clock, Mummy's special time and you need to respect that." The wine is a prop that demarcates the end of the hustle and bustle of the day and the beginning of the grown-up, relaxed affair that is evening. That first glass is the longed-for rendezvous with Mr Unsuitable, after a day spent bogged down with the humdrum of domesticity and/or work.

The regret-laden hangover which presents itself the morning after a heavy night of binge-drinking is often severe enough to warrant a short-lived dalliance with the idea of becoming teetotal, just as an evening spent arguing with your dangerous bad boy lover may cause you to debate the idea of finishing with him once and for all and finding a nice dependable type instead – you find yourself craving some stability and reliability in your life. It's a pleasant thought that makes you feel back in control of your life, and your imagination runs wild for a while with the idea of settling down and being happy and content.

I have lost count of the number of times I considered giving up alcohol, of saying goodbye to my own Mr Wrong. There was the morning after the night when I was so drunk I fell into the (empty) bath while brushing my teeth, banging my head and waking a very unsympathetic ex-partner from his slumber with the crash; another morning when I awoke to the awful stench of hours-old vomit, opening my eyes to see the puke-stained carpet next to my side of the bed, scrubbed but ruined for ever by the bin lid sized circle of orange-coloured sick I had expelled a few hours earlier while asleep; the day after a huge row with an ex had prompted a passer-by to conclude that I was the subject of domestic violence (I wasn't) and to launch himself on my ex in some misguided effort to protect me – the ex-boyfriend wound up being arrested and thrown into cells for the night, the police remaining unconvinced of his innocence despite my drunken protestations of the reverse.

After these and countless other alcohol-fuelled disastrous events I would wake up with an almighty hangover, the pounding in my head soon fading into insignificance as the overwhelming sense of dread and fear rose from the pit of my stomach and began to spread its icy chill throughout every inch of my being. Consumed by self-hatred and remorse I would promise myself 'never again,' make a cup of tea, curl up in front of the TV and wait for the awfulness to subside.

A couple of days later I would be making my next wine purchase and reassuring myself that this time it would be different.

The reasons behind this yo-yoing between heavy binge-drinking and sobriety, of drifting back and forth between a dependable Mr Darcy and the archetypal bad boy Daniel Cleaver (Bridget Jones' Diary) are often down to drama; put very simply, some people like the excitement of it all. The short-lived intention to 'behave ourselves' and quit alcohol never lasts longer than a few days because the steady pace of living alcohol-free seems boring in comparison, and we revert back to our old ways in an effort to reignite the flame of excitement that we feel has been put out.

However, there comes a point in many people's lives when the rollercoaster thrills we welcomed as they hit us thick and fast in our younger years suddenly become tiring, leaving us weary in their wake. The repercussions of a drunken night out are no longer so easy to brush off; the after-effects of our flirtatious, maybe unfaithful behaviour as a result of drinking too much are far-reaching and destructive – lives are being affected and not just our own. Our health becomes more of a concern as we mature and come to terms with the idea of our own mortality and we feel as though something must change; we begin to consider other options. We flirt a little more seriously with the idea of getting our alcohol consumption under control.

A common first step is the intention of instilling boundaries in order to limit the amount we drink, thus putting some damage limitation measures into place. With a wayward boyfriend these limitations might be that we will only see him at the weekend, we will make an effort to cool off emotionally to avoid further dependency, or perhaps we might consider giving him an ultimatum – behave yourself or we're finished.

In replacing the disrespectful lover with alcohol, those same boundaries are equally applicable. Some of my own rules that I attempted to enforce as a regular drinker included no wine when out drinking with friends (large pub measures would usually result in more extreme and rapid drunkenness than if I stuck to beer), no drinking mid-week (except Wednesdays when my daughter went to stay the night at her dad's) and no more than a bottle of wine in one sitting. I never stuck to any of them, and so the madness would continue.

I would also occasionally embark on a 'detox' in the misguided belief that a few weeks off the sauce would aid my poor liver's recovery; the idea that stopping drinking for a month or two can be of help to a damaged liver is nonsense – the only way to avoid alcohol-related liver damage is either to drink very moderately (i.e. sticking to government guidelines) or abstaining completely.

The alcoholic take on 'let's have some thinking space' is not an entire waste of effort or time, however. Living without alcohol for the rest of your life can seem to many people a daunting prospect. Despite the fact that you have a growing awareness of the fact that you and alcohol are a bad match and are destined for a perpetual rocky road, choosing to remain sober permanently can be perceived as a move into scary and virgin territory, and something that you simply cannot contemplate doing for the rest of your life.

A few weeks or maybe months spent without alcohol can bring to the fore all the positives of choosing sobriety as a way of life. Better sleep, improved skin, weight loss, eradication of mood swings, heightened productivity, being a more patient and energetic parent, and feeling calmer and better able to cope in stressful situations are all positive side-effects of not drinking. Perhaps allowing yourself time for a sabbatical from your boozy lifestyle is a good starting point if you know that you need to regain control of your life with regards to alcohol but aren't quite ready to take the big step to a lifetime commitment yet.

If you embark on this short-term approach be sure to keep a record of how living without alcohol makes you feel, including both pros and cons; having a tangible list in black and white to return to whenever you need a reminder can help you put things into perspective, as well as deciding on how to proceed with your relationship with drinking. In the build-up to your temporary break, keep a drinks diary too – people regularly underestimate how much alcohol they are consuming, but by keeping a record of this you are arming yourself with the facts you need when making future decisions.

In regarding alcohol as a particularly undesirable partner we can draw comparisons which should highlight why you would be better off living without it, although you would more than likely have seen these from a mile off if we were talking about an unsuitable human partner.

In a relationship, how long would you be prepared to stand for the following; a lover who repeatedly puts you down and in doing so gradually erodes your self-confidence, one who encourages you to lose interest in any worthwhile activities that you may once have had, who tries to come between you and your kids with the effect that your parenting skills are significantly lessened, someone who encourages you to eat badly and do little exercise with the end result being weight gain and lack of fitness, a partner who keeps you awake at night jibing you with negative thoughts and preventing you from obtaining your optimum eight hours of sleep leaving you irritable and unable to concentrate at work the following day? How would you react if a partner did all of these things to you and in return for this inventory of misery you received only the following positive effects from his company?

The very occasional night of fun, untainted by arguments, jealousy, or any other negativity, and an hour or two of excited anticipation leading up to each rendezvous?

It is likely that you would dump him without a second thought.

In contemplating breaking up with a partner,

particularly one who has damaged our self-esteem, leaving us feeling unconfident and emotionally bruised, we often experience self-doubt and anxieties with regards to the unknown territory of our single futures. Once the deed has been done, however, we rarely continue to suffer such crippling emotional uncertainties and after a couple of weeks pick ourselves up and get back in the race – to quote Frank Sinatra.

After ridding ourselves of an unsatisfactory relationship that has pulled us down for a while and caused much unhappiness, it can be a blessed relief to finally give the son of a b**ch the heave-ho for good. In our new-found singledom, it is not unusual to rediscover the activities we so enjoyed prior to meeting Mr Wrong, meet up once more with neglected friends, buy some new clothes, and enjoy an overall feeling of joie de vivre; and all this when prior to ending the relationship we were terrified of feeling alone and depressed for the rest of our lives!

So, you have endured a rough time with alcohol and you now deem your long-standing emotional crutch to be thoroughly unsuitable and unworthy of your attentions – it's time to move on. Even though life without the prop of alcohol can present itself as a metaphorical leap off a cliff into a massive dark hole, it is important to remind yourself at this point of a very definite truth – things can only get better once you have kicked Mr Unsuitable into touch!

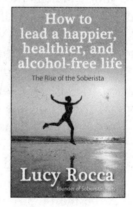